Don't Stay Stuck!

Eliminate Your Excuses and Gain the Confidence to Achieve Your Dreams

*From Teen Mom, High School Dropout, and Field Worker
To 6-Figure Award Winning District Manager*

LORI CHAVEZ-WYSOCKI

ISBN-13: 978-1535069199

Disclaimer

The information contained in this book, along with the complementary resources, is meant to serve as a comprehensive collection of the strategies that the author of this book has applied to get to the next level and earn an extra income. The given summaries, strategies, and tips are only recommendations by the author, and while the author hopes that you will be inspired to take action, there are no guarantees that you will have similar or the same results. The author of this book has made reasonable effort to provide current and accurate information for the readers of this book. Names of colleagues and friends given in the content of this book have been changed by the author to protect their privacy. The author shall not be held liable for any unintentional errors or omissions that may be found. The material in this book may include information, products, or services by third parties. Third-party materials comprise of the products and opinions expressed by their owners. As such the author of this book shall not assume responsibility or liability for any third-party material or opinions. The author will neither guarantee any information, instruction, or opinion of the third-party material, nor shall the author guarantee that you will have the same results as those of the third-party.

The author has taken great effort to ensure the accuracy of the writing and opinions expressed within this book with both personal experiences and the experience of others.

To "My Village" —

My husband, Jeff—who loves me unconditionally, even with all my ideas (some have panned out and others, not so much). Thank you for always allowing me to be me! I know it's not easy.

My children, Alejandro, Amber, Jeffrey, and Victoria—who have had to live with this woman pushing her high expectations and ideas upon them. I am proud of each of you.

My tribe: my stepfather, Steve, my brothers, Victor and Steve, my sister-in law, Tara, and my nieces and grandchildren.

My mom—who did the best she could with the "tools" she had at the time.

I would not be the woman I am today had it not been for all the struggles on this journey we call "life."

Additionally, this is to all of you who feel "stuck" and to the old me.

FREE WORKBOOK

STOP WAITING . . .
GET UNSTUCK NOW!

This workbook is for you if you want to . . .

- Gain **Clarity** about your future
- Get more **Confidence** to go for your dreams
- **Choose** success
- **Create** your own opportunities
- **Connect** with Influences that can help you

What are you waiting for? It's time to take the next step!

Download your workbook at:

www.LoriChavezWysocki.com/freeworkbook

TABLE OF CONTENTS

Acknowledgments

First, I thank my Creator for the breaths that I take each day. No one achieves their goals alone, in my opinion.

I have learned a lot from the struggles I've encountered. When I think back to the crucial conversations that changed the trajectory of my life, oh and there are too many to list, I would like to acknowledge the following:

Althea Anderson—who encouraged me to get my degree and apply for the district manager position. Lem Poates—who insisted I become financially literate. Kem Luck—my dear friend who listened with a tender ear all those years, sitting in her chair at the hair salon, and who prayed for me and with me. Mary Richardson-Davidson—one of my friends who has been encouraging me to write for a while now. Pastors Greg and Becky Marquez—many times I would call the pastor with my problems and his response never changed, "According to your faith, be it unto you." I finally got it, Pastor Greg. Thank you to all the people who have worked for me and with me, and supervisors whom I learned from. To family and friends, you know who you are. And to the many mentors and coaches that I have worked with—I have been blessed beyond measure to have so many wonderful people in my life. To Chandler Bolt, RE Vance, and Ilene Skeen from Self-Publishing School—I don't think it was a coincidence that I heard Chandler on a podcast. You wouldn't be reading this right now without Self-Publishing School guiding me through the whole process of writing and publishing. To my editor, Nancy Pile—who worked some magic. To my writing assistant, Sarah Saucedo (a future author). And, last but not least, my illustrator Heidi Sutherlin—who has been extremely patient with me.

Foreword

A stone lands in a pond, and the ripples jump excitedly from its point of impact. A domino provided the gentlest touch transfers its energy to another and another in an elegant succession that we find both fascinating and wonderfully simple. Similarly, a leader rests her hand figuratively and literally on the shoulders of so many, deserving to be cared for, deserving to be nurtured, and deserving to be challenged. Her impact is a beautiful yet simple succession. A ripple of excitement jumps from that point of impact. The leader, the impact, and the gentlest touch that transfers energy is Lori Chavez Wysocki.

Lori has changed countless lives by challenging people to believe in themselves and to reach for excellence. Lori's leadership has compelled so many to demand the same excellence from those they lead. Spend a day with Lori, and you'll witness several generations of positively impacted people, people who will tell you that Lori not only changed the path of their lives but the paths of their families too.

Thank you, Lori—for sharing your personal story, practices, and beliefs in *Don't Stay Stuck*. You've demonstrated great bravery in revealing the vulnerable parts of your history, all so that others can grow and flourish. I realize that it comes at a price, a price I am so thankful to you for paying so that so many outside your circle can benefit the way so many of us already have.

With much respect and admiration,

Leonard Comma
Chairman and CEO, Jack in the Box Inc.

Preface

My "Why"

I have a lot of people who confide in me and tell me some of their issues as to why they can't achieve certain things when it comes to problems they're facing, not only at work but in their personal lives as well. It amazes me how many people use their problems as reasons for staying stuck.

Quite frankly, I do not take excuses very well. I think excuses hold us back from being all that we can be. However, I do not judge people. Instead, I compassionately listen and let them tell me their stories. Then I gently say to them that the successful person sitting in front of them had a lot of problems at one time as well. Plus, if we are all honest—in life, we're going to have trials and tribulations. It's just part of the journey. It is our response to our trials, be it positive or negative, that has the potential to keep us stuck. I know this from experience, as you will read in this book. However, we can overcome our struggles and move towards the achievement of our goals and dreams; after all, each of us was born a winner.

Come on, let's do this together!

Introduction

Roadblock or Detour?
Your Choice

Over the past few years, I have noticed a lot of people giving up on their goals and dreams due to obstacles or problems that have occurred in their lives. Many of the people I have encountered feel "stuck" when it comes to their problems. However, the good news is that most of these people are completely capable of turning their lives around. People assume that once they are in a certain situation, then that is where they will be forever, with no way out. The purpose of this book is to give you a different point of view on how to take those obstacles and utilize them to push yourself to the next level. I will provide examples of practices, new perspectives, and exercises I have personally utilized in my life to propel me to the next level, even in the face of very challenging, seemingly impossible situations.

I was raised in a single-parent household. I am a high-school dropout. I am a previously divorced single mother, who had her first child as a teenager. Now I am a district manager, enjoying a major leadership position in a company as well as a six-figure salary. I have fabulous children and grandchildren and a loving husband. For these reasons, I believe I know a thing or two about being stuck and pushing your way out. I look back at all the roadblocks in my life and view them simply as detours, similar to having to take a detour while driving because of road construction.

When you encounter roadblocks in your life, although you may get rerouted, you will eventually arrive at your destination as long as you refocus yourself and apply some particular practices, perspectives, and exercises on your new route. It may take a little longer than anticipated, but it is highly likely that you will get there. I use this same philosophy when an obstacle comes into my life or when something bad happens. I do not let it keep me down or stuck.

I often tell people that sometimes you have to take the "back-door approach." The obstacle may cause rerouting or detouring, but when you are persistent, you will arrive, overcome, and achieve your dreams. You can have a great life even when tough times occur; just do not allow those tough times to keep you stuck in a situation such that you miss out on your journey to success.

You have what it takes to succeed—you were born with it!

The Starting Point to Getting Unstuck

If you can remember back to when you were a child learning how to walk—yes, you tumbled and fell, but you got right back up. That childlike faith or belief that you can accomplish things is necessary to succeed. You must believe in yourself. You must tell yourself, "I might fall down, I might have made some mistakes and poor choices, and, yes, circumstances may not have always gone the way I wanted—but I can do this." It all starts with a belief or thought that you can succeed.

This book is similar to hiring a personal trainer, but in this case you will have your very own personal trainer in the form of words. It is an interactive book, packed with knowledge that you can both physically and mentally carry with you wherever you go.

Think about it—if you want a better body, then you go to the gym; if you want better success at the gym, you hire a personal trainer. Other reasons why people hire personal trainers:

1. Personal trainers have the body and muscles you aspire to gain.

2. With a personal trainer, you don't have to spend weeks learning how to correctly use the equipment. You learn how to use the equipment faster, more efficiently, and correctly, so you are more likely to avoid injuring yourself.

3. The best way to speed up time is to find someone who has gone before you and has the credibility based on their results. Then you simply follow their strategies.

In following my guidance to getting unstuck, know you are following someone who has gone before you and done it herself. Know that I've achieved those results you are looking for and that my recommendations are loaded with firsthand experience. I've got the "muscle" and want to show you exactly what to do, so you can unstick yourself from your challenges and enjoy some next-level success ("muscle") too.

Remember that it is during the most tremendous challenges in life, that you will experience the most tremendous growth. This book will help you to experience your desired growth in life.

Your success is only limited by the amount of action you are willing to take. With that said, you will notice that in this book at the end of every chapter, a section will say "Your Turn." This is where you, as the reader and practitioner, take action.

Do not let your roadblocks define you and determine your future. In fact, you may not be aware of this, but *you* are in control of your own life. Your present condition is temporary even if it may not seem this way. Those roadblocks are only detours if you let them be. There is a saying that I use often, "Take those lemons, add some sugar and water, and make lemonade."

Everything in life happens for a reason, so your life challenges can either be valuable lessons to learn from or paths to a greater purpose. It is not the best feeling when you are going through difficult times, but believe me when I say that in many cases, you will look back one day and think to yourself, "I was crying over that?" This has happened to me occasionally. Sometimes, when you experience a difficult situation, you can share it and it can be a blessing to others. This is why I am writing this book for you.

The person I am today is a result of many trials and challenges. I cannot even begin to explain everything, but I will share some of my stories in the hope that you will become inspired to get unstuck and move to greater and greater levels of success.

Chapter 1

The Seeds of Stuck-ness

What lies before us and what lies behind us are small matters
compared to what lies within us. And when we bring what is
within out into the world, miracles happen.
—Henry David Thoreau

I don't think it needs to be said, but to cover my bases, I'm going to say it anyway: just because I'm writing this book does not mean that I don't have issues. I want to inform you that I am still a work in progress. The great news is this: even though I have been knocked down many times in life, I have never allowed circumstances to keep me stuck and take me out of the game of life.

In this chapter, I am going to share with you my earliest "knock-down." I want you to use this story as fuel to rev you up. Analyze how you too can take "knock-downs" that could be considered roadblocks and make them into detours. I want you to be able to take something you might view as disempowering, turn it on its head, and make it empowering for you. It's all a matter of perspective.

* . . . * . . . *

The time was August 1965. I was two-and-a-half years old. My mom, dad, and I were on vacation at Big Bear Lake. What should have been a fun family vacation quickly turned into a tragic family event. This incident became something that marked my life for several years to come.

My mother, father, and I were on a boat, and I remember being so excited to get into the water. I can't recall how long we were in the middle of the lake when my dad, who had been swimming, suddenly started to drown. He tried calling out for help, but because my mom couldn't swim, she could do nothing more than cry and scream for help. Although my mom tried to save my dad by throwing him a towel, towels cannot save lives. I saw my dad go underwater and drown.

I don't recall everything, but I do remember the deck shoes I was wearing because they had monkeys on them. I remember being escorted by an officer who wrapped a towel around my shoulders as we walked up a little hill to a place where we waited for the divers to locate my dad's body.

It wouldn't be until several years later that I would discover that his drowning was caused by a heart attack. He was thirty years old. This was only the beginning of my many experiences with death.

The year of 1968 was a very sad time for my family and our country. My aunt passed away and left behind four children, the youngest one was two weeks old. That same year, there were two major assassinations that would leave our country and my family in a somber state.

You may be curious as to what the underlying message is regarding this information and why it is relevant. Let me explain: I believe you have to take a look back in history if you want to move forward. You must examine some of the events that are causing you to be stuck.

I knew as a young adult that the death of my father was a continuing issue for me, but I could not pinpoint why. When I would go to the beach and look out to the horizon, I would be taken back to that day in 1965. I'd stuffed that tragic event away, and it would only surface as an issue when I was around water, or at least that's what I thought.

Many years later, I have come to realize that although I have been able to achieve a certain level of success, I have always had a certain level of fear. My dad's drowning, my aunt's sudden death, and the assassinations were enough for my then five-year-old self to be abnormally afraid of death for the rest of my life.

These circumstances planted a seed that grew into a beast inside of me. The beast manifested itself in two ways: an excessive fear of death and the need to always feel in control.

The great power of this internal beast was that for years and years I didn't even realize it was there, dictating my life choices.

Excessive Fear of Death: From Roadblock to Detour

It was only after my children became old enough to want to do things away from the house and away from me, with their friends, neighbors, and classmates, that I realized, firstly, that I had an excessive fear of death, and, secondly, that it was posing a serious roadblock for me and my family. For instance, when my children wanted to swim in the neighbor's pool, even though this neighbor was a friend and provided a safe experience for my children, I would freak out. I couldn't handle my children being there and swimming. When my children wanted to go anywhere outside the home without me, I came up with a huge list of what-ifs. *What if you miss the bus and get kidnapped? What if you get hit by a car while crossing the street? What if you spend the night and something happens?*

It might sound like normal motherly concerns, but it really and truly was an unnatural fear that blocked both my own and my children's happiness. I went into this what-if doomsday mode of thinking every day for years. Because my children felt so confined, annoyed, and unhappy about my go-to what-if freak-out response, I was forced to evaluate it, which is how I realized that it directly stemmed from having watched my father drown. From this evaluation, I am now able to understand why I fear for people's safety, so in turn I am able to better manage my anxiety. In this way, I turned a debilitating roadblock into a detour that, with carefully monitoring and managing, I can get around.

The Need to Always Feel In Control: From Roadblock to Detour

Witnessing my father drown also resulted in a desperate need for control on my part. It's reasonable for a person to want control in their life. However, my need for control is beyond the norm. It is urgent and obsessive, so much so, that when it kicks in and can't be satisfied, I become debilitated. And guess what, my friends? You can't control life, so you better believe that I have become overwhelmed and totally vulnerable in my many attempts to control the uncontrollable. Oh, and by the way, it is extremely exhausting and very frustrating for people who see me trying to gain control when it simply isn't possible. Let me give you an example.

I remember flying to San Jose to a Tony Robbins event with my friend Mary. There was some turbulence on the flight, and because I couldn't control the situation in the plane, I panicked, going into total fear mode. Mary must have thought I was having some kind of fit. But there is a silver lining to this story. It was through Mary's response that I was able to change this need for control from a roadblock into a detour. Here's what happened.

Mary looked at me and said it would be okay. Then she suggested I use one of her tips to avoid stressing or worrying while flying. She explained that as long as the flight attendants were moving about the cabin, then I should relax. Only when the pilot asked the flight attendants to clear the cabin and get to their seats, would I have permission to perhaps start feeling worried and recite a little prayer.

I have used this technique to this day. If the flight attendants are moving about, Lori is happy. I know it may sound silly, but the problem simply came down to my impossible need for control and the anxiety it brought me, and those around me when I didn't feel I'd achieved control. I panicked and created a great roadblock between myself and reality, but by recognizing where this need came from, I understand now why it manifests in me so strongly. Through Mary's help, I can now actively manage this need in a much more realistic and helpful way.

I would like for you to review and reflect on your debilitating habits, so you can understand and manage them more successfully. In doing so, you can unstick yourself in situations where you've typically felt stuck in the past.

Your Turn

- A time for reflection: spend a few minutes thinking about situations where you have been stuck and try to figure out where that feeling of "stuck-ness" comes from. This step is very powerful because a tremendous feeling of "stuck-ness" may govern your life, as it did mine. You don't want to go around living in fear and what-ifs, do you? Okay, then start reflecting.

- Once you have done the reflection exercise and identified what "triggers" you, analyze how these "triggers" are keeping you from living life to your next level.

- Now that you know what your "triggers" are that are keeping you stuck, you may have to use what I call PUSH: *Push Until Success Happens.*

Example of a PUSH: In my past, I made it a point to go to the beach and have fun without worrying that someone was going to drown. After I got through the first beach trip, the subsequent trips to the beach got easier. Now I am going to be completely real with you: I don't go out too deep into the water, but I do go deep enough to swim.

You should also know that after my dad died, my mom ensured that I took swimming lessons because she didn't want me to be stuck not knowing how to swim as she had been.

Chapter 2

Choosing Success, Even in a Downward Spiral

Problems are only opportunities in work clothes.
—Henry J. Kaiser

You have to actively make the decision that you want to have a successful life. You must be willing to take the necessary steps to achieve what you deem as "success" because everyone has their own interpretation of what success is.

No matter how difficult your life may become, do not give up on yourself and your pursuit for happiness. Yes, your notion of success may evolve as your circumstances evolve, and that's okay. What must remain strong and steady is your commitment to pursuing your goals.

In this chapter, I'm going to share a personal story to show you exactly what it feels like to pursue your goals even when your personal circumstances are at a low. I'm hoping that my story will give you the inspiration you need to believe in yourself and commit to chasing your goals.

* ... * ... *

I got married at seventeen to a man who was several years older than I was. I hate to admit it, but I had a feeling I was making a mistake even as I was walking down the aisle. We were very different people, with different goals. We were supposed to be happy, but that was not exactly how it worked out. He had his way of thinking as I had mine, and we did not see things eye to eye.

Our relationship became toxic. The disagreements escalated into verbal and physical abuse, which was not a safe environment to raise my children in. However, the best things resulting from this marriage are my two amazing kids.

Since I married at seventeen, I did not graduate from high school and had very little chance to get a good job. I applied at so many places that would provide a good income. I wanted to be able to support my two kids since my husband, at the time, was a farm laborer. However, no one wanted to hire me because I failed to obtain a high school diploma. Because of this, I went on to earn my GED through a migrant worker program since my husband and I worked in agriculture at the time.

After I successfully attained my GED, I enrolled in college courses. At that time, I needed to do something to catch up because my marriage was quickly coming to an end. I decided I wanted to become a nurse because I liked the idea of helping people and felt as if nursing would provide a good salary to support my children.

In the meantime, I applied at Jack in the Box for what I thought would be a part-time job to cover my college expenses. However, as I was headed towards a divorce, I ended up really depending on that job, so much so that I realized I'd better reconceive my attitude towards it. In my mind, it went from being a temporary, part-time job to an opportunity, a road to success. With this new perspective on the job, I ended up staying and growing with the company.

At the time of my divorce, my idea of the path to success was getting my nursing degree, so I would be able to earn a good income and purchase a home for my kids. However, as the years went by and my circumstances changed, so did my idea of the path to success.

What happened was that my supervisor at the time talked to me about seeing Jack in the Box as a career. I gave it some thought. I did like the career path and the benefits the company offered. Also, I really liked the flexible schedule, which is a huge plus for a single parent. I decided to aim to become a restaurant manager while still attending college. In college, I transferred all my general credits that were for nursing to a business degree. As you read farther into this book, I will reveal exactly how far I've gotten on that particular Jack in the Box career path that my supervisor proposed to me when I started in kitchen prep at the restaurant.

Remember that example of a detour? Well, that's exactly what I experienced on my path to success. I had envisioned the way to success one way, but ended up taking a detour to reach it.

The message to you is that your end goal may not come about exactly how you envisioned. So, be flexible and not stuck on one method for achieving your goal. By the way, I eventually bought a house!

So, for right now, decide what it is you want for your life. Decide what your notion of success looks like. Yes, it will likely change and evolve over the years, but you must start somewhere. Do not worry about what others may consider "success" to be or what they have or have not achieved. This is your story!

I want you to be able to have options, and I want you to succeed in this world. One of the many ways to do this is by taking college courses. If you didn't graduate from high school, do not worry. It is never too late to go back and get your General Education Development (GED) diploma if that is what you wish. After obtaining your GED, you have the opportunity to take college courses if you want to propel in that direction.

Whether your goal is working on getting a degree, a certification, or something else, the choice is yours. It is you who decides where you want to be in life, and it is you who chooses the level of success you want to obtain.

A little determination plus discipline will take you a long way. Be a person of your word. My mom and I may have had our ups and downs, but one thing is for certain: whatever you say you're going to do, you must do it. "Your word is like money in the bank," my mom would say, "I should be able to take your word to the bank and get cash for it." She had many sayings, but her most famous is "Pay now or pay later, but just remember that if you pay later, you pay with interest." Think about that one for a while.

Your Turn

- Decide what your idea of success is for your life and go for it. Staying stuck serves no one.

- Determine the very first step you must make to move towards success. Perhaps it is simply doing some research on the Internet to learn more. Perhaps it means visiting a career center. Perhaps it means writing a letter to someone important to you whom you haven't spoken to in a long time. The point is, in order to get unstuck and on the road to success, you must determine what success is to you and the first step towards achieving it. Then do it!

- Do that first step. Commit. And remember, "Your word is like money in the bank."

Chapter 3

Self-Image:
The Success Regulator

Our self-image strongly held essentially determines what we become.
—Maxwell Maltz

In order for you to become the best person you can be, you must work on your self-image, especially if your self-image tank is low!

Self-image is how you see yourself. It is like the oil gauge in your car, but this gauge is about you. If your self-image is high, you are probably experiencing success in your life because you will come across to others as a person with confidence. However, when your car's oil gauge is low, you know you have to get it checked out immediately before you start to have problems. If your self-image tank is low, it is highly unlikely that you will be able to achieve the results you desire.

I have personal experience with low self-image because of the variety of names I was called as a kid. At the time, the words were very hurtful, and after a while, I began to believe what people said about me. For this same reason, I believe that it is important to advertise to yourself with positive "I am" statements, which I will cover later in this chapter and in the "Additional Resources" at the end of the book, but for now, self-image is the governor.

Pity-Party State of Mind

My self-image was so low that I would have my own personal pity parties. I spent a good amount of time and precious energy feeling sorry for myself instead of doing something about it. A "pity party" is a state of mind. When you are stuck in self-pity, it is not a satisfying state to be in. You really cannot get anywhere with that mentality. It is equivalent to running on a treadmill or a racetrack—running and running for so long without going anywhere. If only I could get back all of those years I spent in that place.

I used to blame my mom for <u>all</u> of my problems. *What if she hadn't rejected me? What would it have been like if I'd had a dad growing up?* This list goes on and on, but this mindset did not serve me well, and I have to inform you that it won't serve you well either.

Thankfully, I have great news for you. You can leave this pity party behind if you choose to. I decided to forgive my mother for all I felt she did wrong. When you forgive others, you become freed from the jail inside your mind.

The Forgiveness Gain

Always remember that the one who forgives gains more than the one who is being forgiven. Often, the person you have an issue with isn't aware that there is even a problem. Looking back, I realize that being angry at my mom was a waste of my precious time that I will never be able to get back. I now also realize that she did the best she could with the resources she had at the time. I now find myself telling my grown kids, "Always do the best you can do with the tools that you have." However, I also recommend expanding your toolbox, which is why I'm writing this book—to help people expand their toolboxes by sharing the tools I've developed over the years.

Filling Your Tank

"Where do I go to get my self-image tank filled?" you may ask. Well, that is a great question. It is only you who can work on seeing yourself more favorably. I know firsthand that this is not easy because I, myself, had a tough time filling up my tank.

See, I was never the popular girl in school. In fact, I used to get made fun of and was often called an assortment of names, as I already shared with you. Today this is called being bullied.

Can you believe that I've been called "fish lips?" I laugh out loud about it now with all these girls getting their lips injected—not that I'm against anything a person wants to do to their body.

The name-calling can sometimes get to a person, especially when you're young and don't have the tools or mindset to realize all those names are irrelevant. The conflict is more about the bully's self-image rather than the one getting bullied, but the constant name-calling will bring a person down after a while. For this reason, if I ever got wind of name-calling going on with my children and their classmates and friends, I stopped it immediately. I never allowed my kids to make fun of their peers. Even though a bully may try to bring you down, it is more than likely to be that they have issues within themselves and are taking their anger out on you. This is what I believe to be the truth—it is people who are hurt themselves that hurt others.

If you want to change the results you have in your life, think about this: you have to change your roots if you want to change your fruit. Start by saying nice things about yourself in the mirror daily. "I am smart," "I am a quick learner," and "I am (fill in the blank)" are just a few examples of what you can tell yourself to boost your confidence. I call this "advertising to yourself," just as companies do every time you watch TV or listen to the radio. Use that same strategy and keep saying these great things for yourself daily until you begin to believe that it is true.

Once you believe these things are true about yourself, you will begin to act like it. After a while, you will eventually need to add more "I am" statements to your repertoire.

Let me give you another example of "advertising to yourself" from my son's perspective. During my son's grade-school years, he wanted to enter the Gate class, a special class for the kids with higher grades, or as he would say, "the smarter kids." I signed the paperwork so that he could be tested for the class. Unfortunately, once he took the test, he failed. My son was devastated.

So guess what we did as a result of that? Every day for about a year when I dropped him off at school in the morning, he would say aloud, "I'm taking the Gate test, and it is easy!" Every so often, when I would ask him about the Gate test, he would respond, "I know, Mom, I took the Gate test, and it was so easy."

He took the test again for a second time, and the results came in the mail a few weeks later. He called me at work, asking if he could open the test results envelope. Once he opened the letter, he dropped the phone in excitement because he had successfully passed the Gate test.

Advertising Both to Yourself and the Greater World

"Lori, why do I have to have a good self-image?" I feel that if you don't see yourself as successful, bright, and talented, how do you expect others to see you that way? You may look great on the outside, but if that does not match your mindset and the words you speak, then people will look at you unfavorably and maybe with a bit of confusion.

I remember working in the fields with my ex-husband, harvesting grapes in Sacramento. It was really hot, and some coworkers were talking about how hard things were and how money was so tight. It was not a very positive conversation. I asked myself what I was doing and why I was working so hard in the hot sun. Then, something in my mind clicked.

I knew I needed to find another job, so I started looking and got hired at Del Monte, working in the cannery sorting peaches and tomatoes. From that day forward, I have never called myself "poor." If you see yourself as a "poor" person, then others will perceive and treat you that way. It is a vicious cycle. So if you are saying something that really is not in your best interest, I advise you to STOP NOW.

If you do not work on your self-image, it will be difficult for you to achieve your goals and have the results you are looking for. You can only perform to the level of your self-image. It all starts when you recognize that everyone is unique and we are all humans trying to run our race. There is no other person in the world like you. Remember that nobody has the same fingerprints as you. You were uniquely and wonderfully made! Cherish that and consciously affirm yourself as a unique, wonderful, and capable human being.

Your Turn

- Forgive and be freed from the jail of your mind. You can do this in multiple ways. What worked for me was writing a letter to release any resentment and feelings of betrayal towards my mother. I then burned the letter and moved forward.

- Start a gratitude journal in which you jot down all the positive things you are grateful for. A reminder: if you are reading this, you should be grateful for your eyesight and the ability to read, just saying . . .

- Go to the back of this book and pick out some "I am" statements. Write your own on a sticky note or index card, and put it where you can see it daily. You can also make an alarm or two on your phone to remind yourself to take a few seconds from your day to say your statements. Remember to label the alarm. I still do this.

- Talk to yourself in the mirror daily and tell yourself inspirational things. Inspire and advertise to yourself.

- Check out the picture of my "blessing box" at the back of the book. Anytime I start to even think about feeling sorry for myself, I pull out my blessing box, which is a collection of notes people have written to me, cards from friends and family, and pictures of goals accomplished. It's kind of hard to stay at the pity party with a box full of blessing memorabilia.

Chapter 4

Leveraging Your Passion and Talent

Passion is energy. Feel the power that comes from focusing on what excites you.
—Oprah Winfrey

Once you realize what your passion is and, trust me, you will know once you find it, you can research ways on how your talent can be used in the world. We all have something we love to do, something we do that is unique, something that nobody else in the world can do like we can. You never know, your skill or passion might be something that a big company would be willing to pay for. Maybe you can even turn your passion into a business one day!

You need to leverage your passion for your own good and for the good of others. Discovering your talent and building up your skills can significantly improve your self-confidence. Confidence in yourself can advance you to the next level.

Identifying Your Passion

One way to identify your passion is to figure out what your strengths are. To figure out your strengths, I recommend asking close friends and family to give you feedback on what they think your talents are. This is a good way to gain some perspective because oftentimes other people can recognize strengths you may not have even considered. You might be a great teacher and have a unique way of teaching things to people, but you might not know it. I would suggest trying this exercise to see what kind of feedback you get.

Another way to determine your passion is to think back to your childhood and remember what you aspired to be when you grew up. Then, see if that desire you once had as a child is still the same today. Personally, I have done both.

When I asked my closest friends and my husband what they thought my strengths were, they told me I was very energetic, a great communicator, always positive, and very motivating.

What I am most passionate about puts to use all of these strengths that my husband and friends identified. Also, I am fortunate that I can draw on my strengths and my passion in my work.

You can also use your childhood dream to measure how your current reality is playing out your passion. Let me share with you how I'm doing this. I was always the leader when I was a child when playing different games with my friends. We would play "school" and "library" a lot as children. I always loved to be the boss. It seems only fitting that today I love to read and that I am in a leadership position at work where I get to teach and train.

My work and my passion perfectly align. In my work as a district manager, I get to utilize my passion for teaching every day. Yes, I moved from kitchen prep to district manager. I'll explain how I did that in a later chapter. I also get to recommend leadership books, plus help people in different aspects of their lives, which excites me because that is what I love to do.

Stepping Stones

It is your turn to ask your friends and family for positive feedback. Remember this activity is just to create awareness about yourself. You may be surprised by what your friends and family perceive to be your strong points and unique gifts. Once you have an idea of what you are good at, ask yourself this question, "Would I do this even if I didn't get paid for doing it?" If your answer is yes, that is what I call a passion. Doing something and not worrying about time and money means it is something that you want to be doing, no matter what.

Let me give you an example of someone who is on the path of aligning her work with her passion. Recently, I consulted with Samantha, a young lady who is an amazing makeup artist and has clients that pay her to do their makeup for special occasions. However, Samantha is going to college to get into law enforcement. She looks at law enforcement as a ticket to a good, steady income, which is great. However, when I asked her what she would be doing if money were not a factor, her response was "I love makeup." I then gave Samantha some homework to do, which included finding ways to follow her passion.

Another common situation is when you are already employed, but you hate your job. If you find yourself in this position, do not get discouraged. I recommend finding the things you like about the job and building those skills up while you are getting paid. Let me share with you an example of what I mean.

I had an employee, Grace, who once told me that she hated her job, so I asked her what she wanted to be doing. Grace's response was nursing. I can relate to her because, as you already know, at one time, I too dreamed of becoming a nurse. As a result, I recommended that Grace take over the safety meetings at work. This would allow her to gain experience in working with safety and teaching it to other employees. I also informed her that being a safety coordinator at work would be great for her resume. "I never saw it that way," Grace responded. Instead of being miserable and stuck, Grace is now gaining experience and will be able to add that to her "tool belt." The point: if you look for opportunities, you will find them.

Having a job is a necessity. Jobs can provide you with skills that will help you to achieve your dreams. While I believe studying something you love and finding work that stems from your passion is the ideal, if you find yourself in a less-than-ideal job, you can still use it to grow. There is no need to feel stuck. Just keep in mind this quote from Henry Ford: "It has been my observation that most people get ahead during the time that others waste."

Your job is what you make of it. Here is a tip I use in workshops when people say they can't get ahead in their jobs. I usually ask the same question: "What do you do with your free time?" Most times what you do off the job is what will likely dictate your future on the job. It is a matter of perspective. There is no such thing as a dead-end job unless you see it that way. Look in the mirror and see yourself as a winner. After all, you were born a winner!

Bottom line: discover what your talent or passion is, and use it to serve others. When you serve others, you will be served in return. It is the law of cause and effect, or sowing and reaping. Soon enough you will begin to see yourself differently than before.

A quick note: once you gain self-confidence and a great self-image, and your muscles are strong and you're feeling like a rock star—stay humble. Remember where you came from and always try to help others get to their next level.

Your Turn

- Determine your passion. If you don't already know what it is, one option is to ask friends and family for feedback on your strengths. You will be amazed at the results. Then see if the feedback you received about your strengths aligns with your passions.

- The second option for determining your passion is to recall your childhood dreams for your life. Evaluate those dreams and see if they are still your passions.

- Find or discover ways to use your passion in your everyday life. This could mean making sure the work you do directly corresponds to your passion.

- If you are currently employed, whether you like your job or not, list all the things you like about the job besides the money. Then list all the ways that you can put to use and grow your passion in your current job. Each step is an incremental stepping stone to your growth.

- Take notice and write down everything you do in a twenty-four-hour period. Then analyze where you can make some positive changes and incorporate them to grow your passion in your daily life. You can invest in your time or waste it. It is your choice.

Chapter 5

Birds of a Feather

*Stop letting people who do so little for you control so much of
your mind, feelings, and emotions.*
—Will Smith

I just want to remind you that in life you will often attract
people who are just like you. If you are not happy with
your current circle of influence, you should examine
yourself and how you appear. This point is extremely
important because the people whom you surround
yourself with are often who you become.

Have you ever heard the saying "Birds of a feather flock
together" or "If you hang around dogs, you are going to
get fleas"? This is why when you were younger, your
parents told you to be selective in choosing your friends,
to choose your friends wisely. Notice that you have a
choice (your parents said *choose*) in the matter. You don't
have to stick with the same crowd, or in this case "flock."
This principle applies to your ability to find the
persistence and discipline to make changes in your life
and achieve success. You want to be spending time with
people who are either doing what you are striving to do or
have the higher level of achievement you are seeking to
obtain.

Have you ever noticed that sometimes the people you are
currently spending time with are not prepared to take the

success journey with you? When you go on a trip, you only pack the most important articles for that trip, right? Well, the same applies when you want to achieve your goals, so consider whether those in your inner circle are helping or hindering you on your journey to success. Just because you have decided to be successful does not mean others around you or in your inner circle are trying to get ahead in life as well. Not only that, some of them may feel personally threatened by the changes you are making to reach success. In response, they may make efforts to dissuade you. I have experienced this firsthand, and it can be devastating. Let me share with you a personal story.

Naysayers *Not* to the Rescue

When I decided that I wanted to grow with the organization I was working in, Jack in the Box, I knew one of the requirements was to get a bachelor's degree. I researched schools and determined that I could do it—yes!

However, when I mentioned this goal to a few "friends," they reminded me that I had a husband, three children in school, and a fulltime job as a restaurant manager. So, some of my "friends" let me know how crazy they thought I was, how impossible it would be for me to juggle coursework, and that I should just "settle," or, in other words, "stay stuck." These "friends" communicated to me that I should be grateful for what I had in front of me, which was a good-paying job as a restaurant manager. They wanted me to see that as enough. Additionally, I believe they were probably worried that I wouldn't have time for them either.

For my part, I knew I could do more, that I had more to offer the organization and myself, and that if I made the effort, I could make a difference in people's lives. Even still, my "friends" at the time remained naysayers. They did not act as supporters or encouragers.

You know when you're trying to achieve something "big," you need encouragement. I think that getting a degree was too much for them to conceive as a possibility for themselves, so they certainly couldn't see it as a possibility for me. They underestimated themselves and in turn underestimated those around them—including me.

So what did I do—listen to these "friends" and settle into that life? No way. I pushed through all the negativity. I went ahead and got my degree. Then I climbed higher and higher in leadership positions in the organization, pursuing my path to success. In the meantime, a lot of those friends and I went our separate ways.

The Importance of Being Selective

When you are working on developing yourself, make sure to share your goals with the people who truly understand and can support you. Be cautious with whom you share your dreams as well. Nobody needs a naysayer in their life.

I remember sharing a goal with a friend, and she immediately asked me how I was going to do it in a way that suggested it would be impossible. I went from feeling invincible to feeling stupid for even thinking I would be able to achieve that goal.

Over the years, I have learned whom I can and cannot share certain things with. You too will learn who your true friends are and who your acquaintances are. In summary, try to do your best to surround yourself with positive people. If in your current circle of friends you have no positivity, then I recommend being alone. Yes, alone and positive is better than accompanied and negative.

By continuously working on yourself first, you will develop the confidence necessary to move to your next level. By trying to avoid people who are negative, selfish, or critical, you are more likely to keep your motivation, so you can make the changes necessary to succeed.

Your Turn

- Assess who is on your team or in your circle. If you do not have the right players on your team, then work on getting yourself drafted. You cannot continue to hang around people who are not growth-minded year after year and expect to get different results in your life.

- Once you have determined who the key players are, spend more time with them.

- If you have people in your life who are not productive, positive, and action-oriented, then you may want to kindly dismiss them. I am not saying you need to go serve a professional notice and tell them you can no longer spend time with them. Simply start declining invitations. Also once they realize you have different goals and plans for your life, you then become "boring" to them, and they will slowly go away on their own.

- Another way to gain access to those people who are achieving the life you desire is to read about them. Some of the people you may be interested in reading about might have already passed away, so autobiographies and memoirs are the next best thing.

- When is the best time to take action? Now! So get going.

Chapter 6

Reading Means Expansion

Formal education will make you a living; self-education will make you a fortune.
—Jim Rohn

This is where the rubber hits the road. You see, no one ever told me why reading was in my best interest. And it is in your best interest too to read! Let me share with you what I've figured out.

The "Why" of Reading

I am a firm believer that if you read, you will grow exponentially. You will gain confidence in a variety of subjects as well as improve your comprehension, vocabulary, and knowledge of new facts. In some cases, you will be perceived as an expert since you will have some knowledge about a variety of topics. Once you realize how much reading can positively impact your life, you will want to become a lifelong reader.

Reading can and will open lots of doors because as a reader, you possess an edge that non-readers do not have. When you are speaking to people, they will notice that your vocabulary and comprehension are above average.

Success doesn't just happen to anyone automatically or overnight. It is due to daily, positive habits over a period of time. There is no such thing as an overnight success.

We don't really know how long a person has devoted their time to their craft. You have to begin your success journey somewhere, and reading is a great start because it is something you can take with you—books are literally portable, and the words, knowledge, and wisdom will forever be embedded in your mind.

The "What" of Reading

As I mentioned in the "Your Turn" at the end of the previous chapter, autobiographies and memoirs give you the inside scoop of some of the greatest teachers that have ever lived. When these people lay out their backgrounds, telling where they came from and all the work, setbacks, persistence, and small steps upon steps to their success, you feel like you are there with them, learning to be smart, brave, and disciplined too. It's amazing.

I am currently reading the memoir *Sam Walton: Made In America*. Sam Walton is the founder of Wal-Mart and his story is quite interesting. Unsurprisingly, he wasn't an overnight success and had a few failures, but he pushed through the obstacles.

I think that if you are working on achieving your next level, then you should be looking for books in the genre of your interests and study those books. For example, because my passion involves teaching and leadership, I'm particularly interested in leadership books. I have a collection of John Maxwell books on leadership. I like his simple approach to the subject. My all-time favorite is *The 21 Irrefutable Laws of Leadership: Follow Them and People Will Follow You*. If you are in management, in a leadership position or trying to get there, I highly recommend reading the work of John Maxwell.

I also have an interest in investment strategies, so I have read several books in Robert Kiyosaki's *Rich Dad Poor Dad* series. I like how Kiyosaki's books provoke the reader to think differently.

Additionally, I read for pleasure. I must admit I read the entire *Twilight* series! So, yes, I encourage you to read for pleasure too. It will not only expand your imagination in a way that television simply cannot and increase your vocabulary, but it will give you something to talk about with your children.

If you are interested in keeping up with the latest news, you should try *The Huffington Post* online at www.huffingtonpost.com or Google news at www.google.com. You can even personalize your news on Google so that you can add particular topics that are of interest to you.

Now let me close this section with what I consider one of the best books to have on your bookshelf or Kindle: *How to Win Friends and Influence People* by Dale Carnegie. This book has simple and easy-to-understand strategies. If you work with people, I believe it's a must-read.

The "How" of Reading

Just like with anything in life, investing some time and effort into things is how you grow. You cannot plant a flower and expect it to grow without proper sunlight, soil, water, and fertilizer. The same idea applies to picking up a book and reading.

You must read with intention and the desire to learn something new. Perhaps you will take notes, and if there are any words you don't understand, you can jot them down in a notebook and look them up later.

When I don't know the meaning of a word, I cover it with my finger and reread the sentence to try to figure out its meaning. Oftentimes, this little trick works for me, but when it doesn't, I pull out a dictionary or a thesaurus. After learning the meaning of a word, I make it a point to use it in conversations, so I feel more comfortable using it.

I noticed that after applying this practice for a while, people began to tell me that my vocabulary was great. Between you and me, little did they know that I had just learned that word and added it to my vocabulary.

You must see reading for what it is: a way for you to improve your confidence, self-image, vocabulary, and your whole life in general. Who knows, hopefully once you start reading, you will begin to find it as fun as I do.

Reading's Place in Workplace Success

To show you the importance of being a lifelong reader, let me tell you a story. I recently interviewed Jeremy, a young man who came into the interview dressed very nicely and professionally, which is always a plus. However, during the interview, he struggled at comprehending the questions I asked him. For instance, when I asked how he identified an employee he wanted to develop, he responded by saying that he looks for dedicated, committed, hard workers. As you know, these are pretty much the same qualities. Plus, it was a very generic answer that simply didn't say much.

He also did not have a large enough vocabulary to sell himself. For example, Jeremy repeatedly used a combination of these words: *dedicated, committed,* and *hard worker.* It would have been nice if he'd provided an example. He could have described the person's ability to influence and how they were able to motivate the team to meet the organization's goals, but unfortunately he didn't.

Jeremy's situation highlights the fact that while you can be dressed to the max, when you're unable to convey a message with confidence, logic, and depth, you will most likely not do very well. When no one (like an interviewer, for instance) can follow your reasoning, it is easy to imagine that it will be tough on employees to follow you.

Leadership is really about vision, but if you can't effectively cast your vision and inspire your team, it will be hard for them to achieve the results you desire.

You will find that people who read are usually in higher levels in a company or in leadership positions, earning more money than those who don't read. Try asking the higher management levels in your company how many books they read, and you will be surprised at the answers. I once read an article about a study of CEOs, and statistics showed that most CEOs read, on average, sixty books in a year while the average person struggles to complete one book per year. What this tells me is if you want to get to the next level of success and not stay stuck, you must read and add reading into your daily routine.

I have read over seven hundred books so far in my adult life. My new goal is to read four books a month. Just to prove to you how committed I am (remember how my mom said, "Your word is like money in the bank"? This even counts when you make a commitment to yourself!), I'll share my four books for this month: *The Miracle Morning* by Hal Elrod, *6 Months to 6 Figures* by Peter J. Voogd, *Act Like a Success, Think Like a Success* by Steve Harvey, and I'm still reading *Sam Walton: Made in America* by Sam Walton with John Huey, and the month hasn't ended yet!

You must stretch yourself and your ability to obtain knowledge if you want to grow. What's your reading goal for this month? The good news is that if you are reading this right now, you'll be able to include *Don't Stay Stuck* as a marker on your reading-for-success journey!

Your Turn

- Get a library card. The card is FREE. Once you get your card take a selfie with it, and tag me via Instagram @officialloricw. We'll start our own library card reading movement!

- Go online, read articles, or watch educational content videos that are of interest to you. I recommend: www.upworthy.com for interesting topics or www.huffingtonpost.com

- Go to a bookstore, take in the feeling of being a reader, and buy a book or an audiobook.

- You can also buy a book online and download it to your Kindle if you have one. If not, you can get the app easily.

- Purchase a notebook and use it to jot down the words you have just learned so that you can build your vocabulary.

- Ask a reading friend if they can recommend any books. I get asked this question often.

- Spend fifteen to thirty minutes a day reading. Easy times to read are before going to bed or in the morning. If you want to try the morning, I recommend setting your alarm clock to wake you a bit earlier than normal and reading during that time. Another option is to listen to audiobooks on your commute or to read or listen to audiobooks during your lunch break. Make it a daily routine, whatever works for you.

- Turn off the TV, Facebook, Snapchat, Instagram, Twitter, and other social media notifications for better concentration and uninterrupted reading time.

A "PS" on Social Media

Your time is limited, so don't waste it living someone else's life.
—Steve Jobs

I have surveyed quite a few young people at work and through workshops I have held, and it amazes me how much time people waste on social media and other entertainment distractions. They do not even realize how much time they are spending on social networks until I point it out to them. One young lady responded with the fact that she could get a part-time job with the thirty hours that she spends per week on social media.

You cannot afford to *not* invest thirty minutes a day to read, especially since you're trying to make a positive change in your life. I often ask myself if these people are aware that if they don't change their daily habits, they will continue living below their maximum potentials.

So now I'm urging you—please be aware of your daily habits. Survey yourself. Find the places where you can make positive changes to accelerate yourself on your path to lasting success. Remember the key to not staying stuck is action.

Chapter 7

Educate Yourself

Education is the most powerful weapon, which you can use to change the world.
—Nelson Mandela

Let me begin by saying that I highly recommend and believe in educating yourself, so you can navigate the world with greater ease and success. Even with that said, I don't believe there is one best path for everyone to educating themselves. I think we each have to be smart and deliberate about our education choices. And we each need to consider our own personalities, financial situations, circumstances, and bigger life goals—and work with those when figuring out how we are going to proceed in our own education. Let me explain what I mean by sharing my own journey.

Lori's Rocky Road to Educational Success

High School—I remember asking my teachers why I had to learn certain subjects or skills, and exactly how I was going to use them in the world. They had no real answer for me. This would frustrate me because I wanted to know *why*. I wanted to know more. I wanted to understand the bigger picture.

I think if an educator is looking for an edge in their classroom, they must make a connection between the subject matter and how the subject is going to serve the student throughout their life. The typical answer my teachers gave me did not satisfy my curiosity.

I dropped out of school in the eleventh grade, and I cannot say that I am proud of that either. I did not drop out because I was pregnant, but rather because I felt bored. I could have had ADD and not have known it because they never tested for things like that when I was going through school. What I do know is that I would definitely get bored fast if teachers couldn't find ways to engage me in the materials they were teaching.

I earned my GED through the High School Equivalency Program, also known as HEP, which I was able to qualify for since my first husband was a migrant worker.

College—once I attained my GED, I was able to attend community college and take on six to nine units. I worked with the community college's financial aid advisor to get help on figuring out my options for paying for courses. At the same time, I was taking classes, I was also working and, of course, being a mom. I earned a bachelor's degree in business, and so far it has served me very well.

Was it easy? Hell no. But was it worth it? Absolutely! Getting an education is more than just learning a new subject or material. Getting an education is about who you have to become in order to get through your program to earn your degree or certificate.

I was very fortunate that I was able to take advantage of the classes that were geared towards adults. In my classes there were a lot of students like me who'd dropped out of high school and needed to gain some skills in order to get employed. I was practically dating myself for a while because of how busy I was, trying to parent, work, and gain an education at the same time.

In the end, those classes and long nights helped me to get a good job. I remember taking a typing class, and now I can type pretty fast and am able to use other office machines that were also taught in that class. These classes were not a waste of my time as I still use these office machines today. The classes I took also taught me that my work was a reflection of me and that I should always take pride in my work as it was indeed my reputation.

You Can Do It Too

If you wish to go back to school, but you are working to support yourself and your family, don't worry. You may have to sacrifice a little sleep, but it is possible to go back to school. If you are like me and failed to complete high school, you may need to get your GED, so you can take college courses if you desire. There are many ways to attain your GED, and you will usually be able to work at your own pace.

Moreover, there are many ways to achieve a college education nowadays. For example, you can see if your employer has a program to help you with school. I know that Jack in the Box, Inc. and Starbucks both have tuition reimbursement programs for their employees, depending on the person's level in the organization. The military also has programs to help service members go to college. You can inquire within your workplace to see if there are any programs available.

Traditional Community College

Most cities have a local community college where you can take courses or get a certification at a fraction of the cost of university classes. I attended San Joaquin Delta College where I took the majority of my general education classes. You can go to your local community college to see what steps you need to take in order to enroll. Make sure to speak to a financial aid advisor, as I did, about applying for financial aid.

Online College Courses

If you are currently employed and don't have time to attend classes on campus, do not worry because you can always take classes online. I took online classes while working. Even though it was convenient not having to drive to a classroom and be there at a certain time, you must have self-discipline to be able to complete the course and participate in the online group chats for the courses. Online courses are a way to fit those classes in if you are short on time or want an alternative to going to a campus. Another benefit of online courses is that you meet people from all over and, oftentimes, those connections that were built last far beyond the course.

Other Important Considerations

Because of the typically great cost of college and university educations, I recommend that you be very strategic in how you go about doing it. While high schools used to have career guidance to help students discover their strengths, those specific programs have, unfortunately, been cut from many schools. One consequence of this is that too often, people graduate from high school with no clue about what they want to do with their lives. Having to make that kind of decision and financial investment in education without truly knowing what you want to do is crazy, especially for very young people.

To deal with this, I had my kids both take the Myers-Brigg Personality Type Indicator, a personality inventory, and read the book *Now Discover Your Strengths*. This book comes with an online personality type test, and it provides you with potential career options based on your results. I felt that this was important to do while my children were in high school, so they could get an idea of what their natural bent was in life. No matter your age, I recommend doing the same, particularly if you are planning to go back to school.

Additionally, I have suggested to my kids to first get their general courses out of the way at a junior college while they are still discovering who they are and what they want to do or be in life. To repeat, junior colleges offer courses for a fraction of the cost of universities.

Another place to be strategic is in getting degrees beyond the bachelor's—for example, a master's degree or a PhD. I have seen many individuals go back to school to attain masters' degrees when they have yet to pay off their bachelors' degrees. Call me crazy, but if you have not been able to get an amazing job with your bachelor's degree, what makes you think that you will be able to do so with a master's degree? What about all that debt you are getting into? Once you are finally able to land a job, you are starting off with a huge mountain of debt due to all the student loans you have incurred over all those years of schooling. I recommend that you be smart about it.

Yes, I highly recommend and advocate education. But don't think that if you didn't pursue the traditional path that you've put yourself in an impossible situation. You haven't! Just revisit my own story to remind yourself that with a lot of determination and time management skills, you can get that college education you want for yourself. And again, be smart about it. Be strategic. That way you can minimize your education-related debt and maximize the benefits you get from the classes.

Your Turn

- Determine what it is you need to do to get your high school diploma or GED.

- Take a Myers-Brigg-based personality test online for free to see what your natural ability and skills are or pay for the actual Myers Brigg online test if you would like at www.mbtionline.com. This test will cost you roughly forty-nine dollars. You will find *Now Discover Your Strengths* in the recommended reading section of this book.

  Both of these sites offer similar personality-type tests for free: www.16personalities.com and www.humanmetrics.com

- Ask your human resources department at work if they offer tuition reimbursement programs.

- Contact your local community college for information on attending classes on campus or about online enrollment. Remember you might be eligible for financial aid.

Chapter 8

The Crucial Combo: Work, Money, and Time

It's not resources but resourcefulness that ultimately makes the difference.
—Tony Robbins

We were all programmed to find a job. In school and at home, most of us were taught to get good grades, so we could go to college and get a good job. A lot of us grew up on this theory and idea. For me personally, it replayed in my head over and over again like a song—it must have been a hit!

As I already shared in chapter 4, "Leveraging Your Passion," I advocate that you identify your passion and try to get a job in which you can put your passion to use. Not only will you be highly suited to the job, but you'll really enjoy it and move up higher and higher in the ranks.

Grow Where You're Planted

Of course, I realize that in today's competitive job market, sometimes landing any job at all, passions aside, is a big deal. With this said, I'll return to a point that I made earlier: wherever you start off working, do your utmost to gain experience, develop your skills, and discover your talent. Have you ever heard the saying: "Don't despise your small beginnings"? Even if your current employment is just a pit stop on your way to finding the job that you are most passionate about, it still offers you an opportunity to develop and possibly grow within the organization. You can still do a lot of important learning and growing, so don't dismiss the job as just a place to get a paycheck.

Bloom There Too

The Bible says, "Bloom where you are planted." Just because you started at the bottom does not mean you have to stay stuck at the bottom. You have control over how high on the ladder you want to climb. Your work ethic is extremely important, so don't just work hard when the boss is around. Life is like a boomerang—what you put out, you will get back. So work like you are building the most beautiful structure in the world—whether you are stocking at Walmart or working the cash register at KFC—because, after all, you are the structure.

The beauty of all this is that while you are learning and gaining experience, you are also getting paid. Who knows, you may be able to turn your newly acquired skills into a profitable side business. If you have an entrepreneurial mindset, the sky's the limit. I also recommend finding the path to move up in the organizational ladder while you are on the job. This shows your next employer that you are an upward-and-onward type of person.

My Story: From Food Prep to 6-Figure, Award-Winning District Manager

I have been at my current job for over two decades. Do you remember how I said I got bored in school? While I don't necessarily recommend staying at the same job for this amount of time, it has worked for me because I've been constantly learning and acquiring new skills. Trust me, I wouldn't have stuck it out if I weren't growing so much!

Here's my story. I started at Jack in the Box doing food prep, which is slicing, dicing, and chopping food. Then I would take all of those ingredients and assemble products to be sold. Basically the work was a lot of behind-the-scenes kitchen work. At the time, I was grateful because I was inside and not in the fields.

While I was grateful, to be honest, it was very lonely with all of those vegetables in the back prep area. I'm more of an extrovert, a people person, and in the back of the kitchen I was isolated. I saw how the people at the front counter got to talk to customers as they took their orders and money. So I kept my eye out for a way to "graduate" to cashier.

I asked a coworker how the register and counter worked, and she showed me how it was done. Then whenever I got my work in the back done, I would make my way to the front of the restaurant to help. Not only did this show my boss that I had initiative, but it got me out of being the prep person and into the front of the restaurant. Oh, did I mention that the prep person has dish detail too?

I learned the cashier position and did it very well—remember, the customer is always right! Right? Eventually I basically got bored with the register and moved to all the various positions of the kitchen. Then one day my restaurant manager asked me if I would be interested in being a team leader. I responded that, of course, I was interested! Their uniforms were much nicer, and they didn't have to wear a hat. No more hat head for me! Plus, I got a pay increase. I was able to accomplish this in three months.

Remember, too, that I was going to college at the same time and I was a single mom. So at that time I thought to myself that I would prefer being an assistant manager because their schedules were better, the pay was better, and there was bonus potential, sick time, and vacation pay. I asked the current assistant managers in the restaurant what they did and how they did it, and then I informed the restaurant manager of my interest in becoming an assistant manager.

After six months of training, the day arrived for me to be certified, meaning I had to demonstrate my ability to manage the restaurant. I was a bit nervous, but I passed and got the promotion. I remember I was very excited at the time because I was moving up. I stayed in that position for almost five years because there was no growth in the market that I worked in, meaning they weren't building restaurants.

Meanwhile my district manager at the time kept dangling the "carrot" of becoming a restaurant manager. My becoming a restaurant manager didn't come about how I'd expected. In fact, I actually moved to a different city across the state because my current husband got hired with the department of corrections. So while this was great for him, I had to start all over, well at least that was what I'd thought.

When I got to the new restaurant, my supervisors really didn't know what to do with me, so they transferred me to various restaurants within the district. Because of my work ethic, I got recognized pretty quickly. I was transferred to a different restaurant in September, and by February I had gotten promoted to restaurant manager because I'm extremely growth-minded and an avid reader. I consumed so many leadership books and found many ways to inspire my crew.

I stayed at the restaurant manager position for about sixteen months, and then I was promoted to general manager, which entailed supervising two locations.

As a general manager, I remember having a meeting with my assistant managers from both locations and casting my vision. My intentions were applying for the district manager position and going back to school to earn my bachelor's degree. I explained to them that while my intentions were to move up, I wanted to know which one of them wanted to grow to the restaurant manager position and take my two spots.

Let me pause in my story to explain that you always want to have someone who can fill your shoes. You never want to miss out on getting a promotion because there is no one ready to take your place. In this way, it is beneficial to help others along your journey. Always have a succession plan in place.

Once I received my bachelor's degree, I did get promoted to district manager. I started off in charge of twenty-one restaurants in two states and three counties, although since then, the company has reduced the span of control to eight to twelve restaurants. The district manager position didn't come easy as I will discuss in the "Never Be Afraid to Be-Live" chapter. Sometimes when I think back on my career path, I couldn't in my wildest dreams have imagined going from the prep position, earning two dollars and ninety-five cents an hour, to becoming a district manager and earning over six figures a year, including bonus pay and the many trips and awards I have received.

I have enjoyed the district manager role for many reasons, among them because of its very flexible schedule that allows me to pursue other interests that keep me growing and developing. Do you see the correlation with learning and earning? I have taught part-time at the local community college as an adjunct instructor, consulted, and have been asked to be a guest speaker. This is in addition to my fulltime job. You see, my passion is to help people, and as long as I'm breathing, I intend to do so.

More Clutter vs. More Options

Once you get promoted and start to earn more money, do not promote your lifestyle. What I mean by this is just because you start earning more money, don't start spending more on material possessions. Instead, use a little of the extra income to invest in yourself. For example, you can take a much-needed online course to attain a new skill or certification, hire a coach, or attend a conference. There are many ways to invest in your personal development.

Keep your goals in mind and save, so you can use the extra income to achieve your goals. That extra income might be used to take a photography class or buy a better camera lens so that you can improve your photography skills and land more side jobs.

Remember that it is your personal development that will lead to even greater increases in your salary and career options. Plus, your own development will likely make you feel happier, more accomplished, and less stressed out. Please, please, please, remember to have a plan on how you'll spend your money (i.e., invest in yourself), and be sure to follow it.

Don't spend the extra money you are earning with no plan in mind; otherwise, all you have gained is just more things, more clutter, and clutter will keep you stuck.

I made this mistake early on when I didn't consider the big picture. Don't get me wrong, my job has afforded my family a comfortable life, but this life came at a cost and that cost was my time. Let me explain.

The Currency More Important Than Cash

Increasing your lifestyle as your income increases (spending your increased income on material items) is self-sabotage. You don't want to be working more and more in order to just maintain a lifestyle. For one thing, you'll be spending so much time at work that you won't even be able to spend significant time with those new possessions you've accumulated.

I believe time is a currency, which you can spend or invest, but once spent, you will never get to recover it. This is why I like to invest my time efficiently. When I learned about the importance of time, I developed a plan that shifted things in my life in regards to my time and money. I have been able to use my income from my job to create other sources of income from things that I am passionate about. These investments have benefited my family just as much as they have benefited me. For example, I have saved bonus income to invest in real estate. My rental property produces a cash flow income each month in addition to offering a tangible asset for my kids when I'm no longer here.

I constantly try to find ways to multiply my time by ensuring that I teach others how to do things. I taught one of my sons how to write checks and pay bills (yes, I signed them) when he was in high school. I think it is important for a young person to learn how to write checks and record them in the ledger of the checkbook. Now I know that online banking is a popular way of paying bills, but I wanted him to have the principles of managing money and paying bills. Most high schools don't have home economics classes anymore. Also by teaching my son to do this task, I no longer had to take my time to do it, thus multiplying my time. There are many tasks that should be delegated to your youngsters as it helps prepare them for when they leave home.

This is what I'm recommending to you: evaluate what part of the day you are most efficient and have the most energy. When you become aware of your peak energy zone and understand how important it is to achieve your daily results, you can schedule certain tasks when you are at your peak. In other words, you don't want to wait until the end of the day to get certain projects done if this is not your most efficient energy zone. This way you know when it is the best time for you to get certain tasks done.

If you don't think managing your energy is important, remember that you exchange energy every day. Someone is "renting" your energy in exchange for money. This is what a job is, essentially! This is why it is extremely important to make wise decisions with your time and income. Think about it for a minute—your money is a clear exchange of your energy because you can't buy time.

Avoiding the Debt Trap

To repeat, always determine whether or not you are acting your wage or trying to live above your wage. Your job should provide you with a way to pay your bills and hopefully enough for you to save or invest in your dreams. You don't want to fall into working many, many hours each week simply to accumulate possessions—or even worse, to accumulate possessions and a whole bunch of additional debt.

Why does a person fall into a debt trap? I believe because we want everything so quickly, instant gratification. We want a new car, television, or the latest cell phone. Because credit is so easily available to everyone, it is easy to fall into the debt trap. The debt trap is often the destroyer of dreams since it keeps us distracted and perpetually behind—as it takes forever to pay off the debt we accumulate.

Let me add that if you are financially stuck in a situation, don't worry—you will learn more in the "Funding Your Dreams" chapter.

Self-Development & Real Job Security

If you think you have job security, think again. I'll explain myself with a little story.

I was recently chatting with Henry, a former employee who landed a job in the irrigation sector, which provides water for farmers to water their land. Henry was excited to tell me about his new job and all of the benefits of his new position. In response, I told Henry how excited I was for him and how it was a really great company.

However, I did have to be honest, so I asked him to tell me a little more about his job and the job security that he insisted he had. I then asked him one question that changed his thinking, "What happens if or when El Niño hits or when it rains a lot?"

Henry replied, "Well, I guess my hours will be reduced."

I then stayed quiet. He proceeded to tell me how he hadn't thought of it that way.

None of us have real job security. We are all susceptible to getting terminated or laid off due to unforeseen circumstances. With positive intentions, all I wanted was for Henry to think about the big picture. Sometimes people don't or can't see the big picture, and I wanted to make sure that Henry understood, so he would be okay in the future.

Although I may sound like a naysayer, I aspire to help you think and become prepared. When you are prepared, you will be able to weather all the storms of life a lot better. This is why I teach people that you must go out and make your own job security. That's why you should invest your extra income on your own development and avoid the instant gratification trap. Do you really need the latest smart phone or a new car? Give yourself skills so that you have options. I'm not saying you can't have nice things because you can. What I'm saying is be smart about it.

For example, I purchased a pre-owned BMW, and while it was a really great deal and was amazing to drive, it wasn't the best purchase due to all the maintenance. For my work, I drive across two states and put lots of miles on my vehicles. So, I had to be smart about it, and I eventually went back to a more practical car for my type of job.

Remember to develop yourself and choose wisely. Make your own job security!

Your Turn

- Find a job at www.indeed.com or www.linkedin.com. Use LinkedIn to keep track of your work history and easily build your resume. Ask your previous supervisors for recommendations.

- I don't know how many times I hear, "I got hired part-time, seasonal." My response is always: go in there and rock their world because that part-time can turn into fulltime with benefits. No employer is going to allow an exceptional part-time, seasonal employee to leave their organization. Remember, your gift makes room for you, but you have to be a gift to the organization first.

- Learn as much as you can about the industry you are trying to get into. If there is a skill you need to learn in order to get the job of your dreams, take a class or research a way of adding that skill to your resume. For example, if you need to learn how to speak Spanish, you can either take a class or two, or invest in a program like Rosetta Stone. Go to this site to learn more about it: www.rosettastone.com

- Write down what you love, plus any experiences that you have gained from your job, and find a way to turn that passion into profits.

- Continue to work daily on your dreams and goals, and remember—there is nothing you can't do if you get your habits right!

- Avoid the instant gratification trap. I have been cured of the shopping bug. I now ask myself whether the item is worth purchasing and pushing my goals aside for. I have a rule in my house when purchasing clothing: no tags come off the clothes until you're going to wear that item. I want the option to return an item, especially if it was purchased on an impulse. I don't know how many times I would find stuff in the closet that I had never used and, therefore, wasted money because I had no tags to return it. Also, after a few years, no store is going to give you your money back for it.

- Volunteer work is a great way to gain skills and experience, and you will feel great doing it. Plus, it looks great on your resume.

Chapter 9

Fast-Track Your Success by Finding a Mentor

A mentor is someone who sees more talent and ability within you, than you see in yourself, and helps bring it out of you.
—Bob Proctor

Whatever your passion may be, find someone who is doing what you desire to do in your life. A mentor has the knowledge and experience that will help you eclipse time, so you can reach your goals faster. Once you have identified this person, ask if they would be able to work with you as your mentor. Be prepared for possible rejection based on the person's personal projects and busy schedule, but don't let that bother you. Keep looking.

Who

There are a few ways to come across mentors. You can find someone in school, a successful family member, or someone at church or even at work. The person you are asking oftentimes will be flattered by the fact that you think so highly of them.

I believe it's important to find a mentor who has achieved some level of success in the area you wish to excel in. There are a lot of benefits to having someone guide you and hold you accountable.

What

Once you find a mentor, they will usually want to have a conversation to get to know you and what you are looking to accomplish. After you have determined what course of action to take in terms of length of time to achieve a goal or an ongoing tune-up, you will agree on a schedule and set up your appointments. Back in the day, consulting with a mentor was all done over the phone, but as we have evolved, it is not unusual to have meetings through Skype. I actually prefer Skype because you can see your mentor or coach.

The meetings typically run sixty minutes. So you will want to ensure that you are on time, prepared, and that you will have no interruptions. If you made a commitment to get something accomplished before the meeting, don't come back with an excuse as to why you couldn't do it. Remember, this is time for you to grow personally and professionally, so do your best to accomplish your commitments.

I remember when my mentor assigned me a task and I didn't complete it. He then reminded me that I was wasting his valuable time and my money. He paused, and I knew it wasn't good. I wasn't mad because I wanted him to hold me accountable, and I did not let it happen again. Learn from my error and be ready to go. Also, remember to turn off your cell and other distractions, for this shows your mentor how important their message is.

Me and My Mentors

Lem Poates was a significant mentor in my life. He started me on the path to financial literacy. Lem was my supervisor for a very short time, but became my mentor and someone who had great financial acumen. Plus, he had the results.

Lem's financial guidance began when he handed me a bonus check and I did the happy dance as I told him I was headed to the mall. On that day he insisted I make him a promise to make an appointment with his stockbroker and friend. I wasn't too thrilled at the time, but I did it anyway.

When I walked into the stockbroker's office on the very top floor of the building, I was nervous, thinking, "What have I gotten myself into now?" We chatted for a bit, and she asked me what my financial goals were. I ended up feeling great about the appointment. Just a couple of weeks later, my husband and I opened an account.

Lem and I spoke regularly about stocks and investments. He spoke to me at my level since I had not, at that point, acquired any financial knowledge. Unfortunately, Lem passed away shortly after. But his investment of time and knowledge has helped not only me but also many people that Lem never met. This is what I call a legacy. Thanks, Lem!

Professional Development Coaches

I have hired personal development coaches for over fifteen years, and this has benefited me as I continue to grow and develop. Remember—you want to be a lifelong learner. There is something powerful about having someone assisting you and holding you accountable to your goals and dreams. I see investing in my development as a need and not a want.

I hired a coach to help me get into the right headspace when I was managing sixteen restaurants in two states. I was feeling overwhelmed, so I hired Lisa to help me accomplish my goals. I didn't want to be an average district manager, but I couldn't do everything. Plus, I had kids at home. Lisa and I discovered that the ugly head of "control" was trying to pop up. Yes, remember, I already said I was a work in progress.

My coach helped me to see delegating in a different light and to choose someone I could develop and trust. Then she helped me see how the tasks that I would be delegating would provide experience for this individual and that it would be a win-win situation, for my coach knew I loved to teach. We developed small steps for me to take and eventually bigger steps.

Needless to say, I listened to Lisa, and at the year's end, it was announced that my team and I had achieved the Circle of Excellence Award, which is not that easy to accomplish when your district goes through periods of realignments.

I know you're thinking, "I don't have the money to invest in my personal development right now," but there's something you need to know. There are plenty of people who volunteer their services. Additionally, there are government agencies and nonprofit organizations that offer free personal development services. The key is to take the time to do some research to find the local and online services that are available, either free of charge or practically free of charge. You have to become aware that there is a service available to you.

The Value of LinkedIn

I also recommend using LinkedIn. LinkedIn is what I call the "professional Facebook." Once you have an account with LinkedIn, you can follow groups in various industries and maybe even find a mentor or a job. Once you begin following these groups, you will discover the language that is used in that particular sector.

Every industry that I have ever been a part of has its own language. When I studied nursing, the "-itis" at the end of a term meant some sort of inflammation. In the restaurant industry when you hear someone say "eighty-six," it means they have run out of that item. In the financial world, you will hear "compound interest," which basically is the interest an investor earns on the original investment plus all the interest earned on the interest that has accumulated. In the horse world, when you hear someone say they are going to "tack up," they mean they are going to saddle their horse. (I learned a lot about horses when my youngest daughter started riding!) Every industry has a language, and unless you learn that specific language, you will not be able to navigate in that industry very successfully.

I recommend getting on LinkedIn, so you can become familiar with the language of a particular industry. This will also give you an edge as you become familiar with the industry and begin to make certain connections.

As John Maxwell said, "Your network is your net worth." As you embark on your journey to success, growing your own personal development, skillset, and education, you will be expanding your network. In turn, this will increase the value of your collaboration into projects, meaning you'll know more, be able to do more, and be able to think more broadly and deeply, so you'll eventually earn more.

What is so fabulous is that maybe one day you will be in a position to pay it forward and take someone under your wing. You might be able to mentor someone else or be a part of someone else's network to grow that person's net worth.

I'm imagining this as the "Don't Stay Stuck Movement." It sounds great, right? We should all be willing to pass on the knowledge of how to get unstuck from situations to help others.

Your Turn

- Find a mentor because rarely will you be able to achieve your dreams alone.

- Ask someone who is in a position that you would like to be in if they would be willing to help you.

- If you are looking to get into a different position in a company, always ask questions and always ask the right people for help.

- Create a LinkedIn account: www.linkedin.com

- Ask others who are successful if they have a resource that they can recommend to you.

- Always remember to thank your mentor for their time. Remember, they will never get back the time they invested in you, so take advantage of what they have to offer you. Take notes, and apply what you learn to your life.

- Explore the government agencies and nonprofits in your area to find which ones are offering personal development and coaching services. Be sure to examine their offerings online and also visit the places in person.

- Toastmasters is another way to gain communication and leadership development. This group offers you the opportunity to practice public speaking. To lead a group of people, you will need to be able to do public speaking. Public speaking freaks most people out, including me at one time. You can find your nearest Toastmaster club online at www.toastmasters.org.

Chapter 10

Got Goals?

Write the vision; and make it plain on tablets, that he may run who reads it.
—Habakkuk 2:2

One of my defining moments happened at church when I heard my pastor's message about Abraham and Sarah. It was when God told Abraham to look up to the sky that he would be the father of many nations. My aim is not to force my religion or faith on you, but what I got from this message was that God told Abraham to look up to the sky to give him a visual that he, Abraham, would be the father of many nations and the stars that he looked up to represented this. Basically, it is an encouragement to visualize the most positive outcomes for yourself, to see them as true and real. If it was good enough for Abraham, it is good enough for me.

In addition to visualizing, I have another powerful action step for making your goals happen. It is what I call "chunking." This is how chunking works: write down your goal in the middle of a paper, circle it, start to think of all the smaller steps that must be done in order to reach that goal, and write down everything you can think of. It's a mind map, if you will. What I've found is that when you take a big goal and break it down into distinct, small steps, then it is easier to achieve.

In addition to chunking, there is a variety of methods for achieving goals. I will share a few. No matter the method though, the first thing you must do is decide what you want to achieve.

SMART

SMART is an acronym for *specific, measurable, achievable, realistic*, and *time-bound*.

So, let's talk about how to use George T. Doran's SMART method. First, I write down my goal on a sheet of paper, and I make sure to frame my goal in terms of the five characteristics given in the acronym. An example of a SMART goal is: I will read one self-development book a month for the next year. The reason this goal is SMART is that it meets the five criteria of the acronym. An example of a goal that is *not* a SMART goal is: I will make a million dollars this month. While this goal is specific, measurable, and time-bound, it is not exactly realistic and achievable.

Next, I take that goal farther by recording the SMART goal on sticky notes or index cards that I tape to the dashboard of my car and on the back of my restroom door.

Why these places? You want to put the reminders where you spend a lot of time daily. We do spend some time in our bathrooms daily, so in this way we will be constantly reminded about our goals whenever we use the bathroom.

I'm sorry, but I have to be honest and tell you what I do. So go ahead and laugh, and then do it. Come on! Tell me you don't take your cell phone to the restroom with you. If you do, make sure your screensaver is a picture of your mind map or your SMART goals.

You should use the same strategy that big advertisers use to get us to purchase something whenever we see the commercials on TV. That strategy is simple: they constantly show us the item, constantly advertising its perks and advantages, so we can be influenced into buying it. You must keep your goals in front of you at all times. By visualizing the perks and advantages of achieving the goal, similarly to what God told Abraham, you are influencing yourself to make it your reality.

Dream Board

I also use a dream board to help me to visualize my dreams. The more real I can make my dreams through distinct images, the more motivated I am to make them into reality.

To create a dream board, all you do is go on the Internet or find some magazines with pictures of your goals. For example, your goal might be to purchase your first family home, so you can find pictures of houses. Then you cut or print them out, and paste them on your board. Then you have those images to look at daily, which will help you to make the appropriate decisions to achieve that dream.

Another example: if your dream is to be able to master post-production photo development skills in order to make extra money by digitally tweaking people's photographs, then you should look for images of cameras, computers, people working from home, as well as digitally-altered images. All of these will remind you of your dream and would make a powerful dream board.

After making a dream board, do not expect all your dreams to come true automatically without taking steps to achieve your dreams. That will not happen. The key to a dream board is to remind yourself what your desires are and to constantly advertise them to yourself. The idea is that you have to physically see your goals multiple times a day in order to take action—the same way the TV delivers the same commercial over and over in hopes of convincing you to purchase an item.

When I make a dream board, I post it up on my refrigerator. This can be tricky depending on whom you're living with. If you live with positive people who inspire you to reach for your dreams, then I am sure you will have no problem. If you live with people who are not as positive or ones who will judge or put you down, then posting your dream board publicly is probably not a good idea. You want to surround your dreams with positive people, people who believe in you, not people who are constantly negative or putting you or your ideas down.

Another practice I do when visualizing my goals is to take a picture of my dream board and set it as my screensaver. The key is to review your goals often during the day, before bed, and first thing in the morning. This can be another way to advertise to yourself.

I believe in keeping your dream board manageable to start with. You can begin with a handful of goals that you would like to attain. For example, you wouldn't want to start with getting a PhD. It's too much. It would make more sense to start with a bachelor's degree. The reason why is that incremental success is very motivating. The easier and more likely success you could achieve with earning a bachelor's degree propels you to achieve another step on the path to the bigger goal of a master's degree, thus making it a greater likelihood that you'll achieve your doctorate.

Once you gain the confidence and results you desire, go ahead and add more to your dream board. I recommend keeping it simple and starting with more attainable goals so that you can get some wins under your belt. The confidence boost from some small wins will increase your determination, energy, and focus for achieving the bigger goals down the road. Using this method is efficient and serves as a steady reminder of what you desire to achieve.

My Dream (Board) Come True

Once I wrote down exactly the type of home and price point of a property I wanted to purchase to turn into a rental property. Then I became very clear with the belief that it would happen. One Sunday after church, I was reading the real estate section of the newspaper, and there was the property I wanted with all the specifics. Another example is when I decided to buy a vacation condominium. I cut out a picture of a nice property and posted it right next to my bed. It was not long afterwards that the townhouse came into my life. I have done this with different places around the world that I would like to visit as well.

Notice that nothing magical happened in my examples. I still had to make efforts to turn these dream boards into reality. But the image or the word description reminding me daily of my goal certainly motivated and focused me. You too can take any goal you aspire to achieve and advertise it to yourself, as long as you stay motivated and take consistent action towards its achievement.

The Be-Live Factor

I take the word "believe" and pronounce it "be-live." I feel that as long as I want to do something with my life, I first have to become it and live it in my mind before it can make its way into my life; hence, "be-live."

I'll explain my use of "be-living" in achieving goals through Jim Carrey's example. I once saw how Jim Carrey, as a young, aspiring, no-name actor, wrote himself a huge check for "acting services rendered." He post-dated the check ten years. It was his way of putting his belief into action. Every time he would open his wallet and see the check, he advertised to himself. He "be-lived" it, so he did it. It takes action, whether to become a famous actor or a homeowner.

You may ask, "Lori, how do I 'be-live' these things?" Think back to a time when you achieved any goal, big or small. Now recall how that goal started. Your goal started with a *thought*. You thought of it, wanted it, and then you took the necessary steps to achieve it.

Say my goal is to become a landlord, but I have no clue of how to accomplish that. The solution is to read books on real estate, study it, and research it. I must gain some knowledge and then put that knowledge into practice. Maybe I will interview current landlords and ask questions to gain more insight. Perhaps I will talk to a few real estate agents. Once I obtain the knowledge of what landlords do, I can now add this information into my character of acting as a landlord.

My Be-Living

I put this same practice into place several years ago when I wanted to become a district manager. Being a district manager requires a very different skillset than running just one or two units. So once I decided on my goal, I needed to study and research it. Then I asked other district managers a ton of questions at every opportunity I had. With that information, I proceeded to act like a district manager while running just two units.

Although I'd thought I was fully prepared for the new district manager position, I was rejected in my first interview. Post interview, I got asked to supervise the district while they continued to search for the right candidate. Out of pride I could have easily refused and had a bad attitude. However, I knew that I was able to do the job and that I had a chance to be the district manager for the company, even though it was only a temporary position.

Long story short, I began managing temporarily the twenty-one restaurants in the district in April 1998. In October of that same year, I earned the district manager position permanently. I didn't allow the circumstance of not passing the interview the first time to keep me stuck. I went on to be one of the top, award-winning district managers in the company.

You see, just because you do not achieve your goal the first time around does not mean you should give up on your dreams for the future. You must continue to "be-live" and make any and all adjustments you can to achieve your goals and your dreams.

"Be-living" your dreams is equivalent to attending a college and having to take a prerequisite for a class. It is the stepping stone, the beginning point that will soon lead you where you want to be.

Be-Live Your SMART Goals

Let's explore SMART goals even more, so you can better harness the concept to achieve your goals. Also, we'll combine SMART goal setting with my practice of be-living goals in order to set you up to make a lot of progress on achieving the goals you set for yourself. Remember that SMART goals are *specific, measurable, achievable, realistic,* and *time-bound.*

Part of being a SMART goal is that the goal is *measurable*, meaning that you can actually measure your overall progress toward achieving it. The most common measurable goal is weight loss because you can step on a scale and physically measure the progress that you are making throughout your journey. You can also measure your progress by noticing when your clothes begin to fit loosely. Obviously, once your clothes are too big, you know you have lost weight. If it's not the clothes that are shrinking, it must be you!

In order for a goal to be *achievable*, you must break down or chunk the goal so that it is easier for your mind to perceive the possibility of attaining it. Basically, how would you eat something as big as an elephant? Your answer would be—one bite at a time. You sometimes have to take your bigger goals and break them down into smaller steps in order for them to become achievable. That way you won't become overwhelmed by the single big goal and can instead look at the very doable pieces of it. By doing this, your brain doesn't give up on you.

I have found that breaking down goals into smaller steps is how you will gain the greatest belief and confidence that your goal is in fact achievable. Once you have this confidence and belief, you are more prone to take action towards your goal. Never underestimate the importance of gaining self-confidence because confidence is the elixir to achievement.

Writing a book is a good example of the power of chunking a big goal. If you wish to write a book and you want it to be around 25 thousand words, it is easy to become overwhelmed at just the thought of it. You can get so overwhelmed that you may never begin to write your book. However, if you tell yourself to write at least five hundred words a day for five days per week (so this is the chunking part of it), then you should have your rough draft ready in ten short weeks.

Take any goal and break it down. Once you break down your goals, they soon become not only more achievable, but they also become a lot more *realistic*. Realistically setting your goals is another step in goal setting when using the SMART system. When your goals are more realistic, your mind is more likely to decide to take the necessary action to achieve them. For example, if your goal is to be a dentist in two years, but you have yet to take any classes or courses to learn about dentistry, then more than likely your goal is not realistic.

On the other hand, if you want to be a dentist and you have done research on what it takes to become one and have determined how many years it will take to meet all the requirements, then you've made your goal more realistic. In turn, you are more likely to achieve that goal.

Why? Because you have established a realistic timeframe for the process and you know all the steps involved. It might be a long process, but if you have the steps written down and understood, you can easily break down those steps into smaller steps and begin to do those one by one. Before you know it, you are already on your way to dental school.

Another important characteristic of SMART goals is that they should be *time-bound*. There are some goals out there that may take a long time to complete, as in the example of starting from zero to become a dentist years down the line. By setting a date for achieving the goal, you make it more manageable to achieve and can motivate and measure yourself based on that. You can even set yourself smaller steps you must take to get to your overall goal. This will lead you to becoming more driven to get your specific goal done by the specific timeframe you determined for yourself.

For example, say your goal is to purchase a car. First, decide what model of car you want, what year, and how much you are willing to spend. Let's say you want to purchase a Honda Accord and want it to be five to seven years old. From here, you should start searching for what the particular model is selling for online or go to a dealership nearby. You find out that you can get a Honda Accord for approximately $5,000. Knowing that you have

$1,400 saved, you now know that you need to save $3,600 more.

The next step is to decide how much you can save per week. Let's say you decide that you will save one hundred dollars per week or $400 per month. Now you know it will take you nine months to achieve your goal of purchasing a Honda. You may also want to consider taking on an extra part-time job, or you can also use your tax returns and add that to your Honda Accord savings account.

I used this same example when I wanted to purchase a BMW X5. First, I went online and found a couple of pre-owned vehicles that were in the price range that was in my budget. Next, I went to San Diego to test drive one of these cars and to get myself into the mindset of "be-live." As you can see, I use the "be-live" strategy a lot. I believe that if you put yourself into the desired position as closely as possible, it will become easier for your mind to believe in yourself. When I test drove the BMW, I took pictures of myself inside the car, so I could look back at them and reminisce about that feeling.

Time Investment & Goal Achievement

It amazes me how many people waste time when time is each person's most valuable asset in life. We all have the same twenty-four hours in a day and 168 hours in a week to invest in. If people start to think of time as money, then maybe time won't be wasted as easily and often as it is now.

I have done many workshops where I interviewed the participants about time, and it amazes me how people will say that they don't have time to complete a simple goal. When I asked them how much TV they watched in a day or how much time they spent on social media, often they didn't realize the amount of time wasted that could be invested in goal achievement. I share this to encourage you, once again, to take a good hard look at your day-to-day practices and choices so that you can make sure you are doing the most you can to achieve your dreams. It's not just identifying your dreams and visualizing them alone—it is harnessing your time and energy in order to act that is required to achieve your dreams.

In one of my workshops, a young lady shared that she wanted to become a teacher. I then asked her for clarification on the "wanted." She then stated how she wanted to but knew it was going to take a long time to become one. In other words, this young lady was already giving up on her goal of teaching before she even started because she wanted to do something that was quicker.

If this young lady's dream was to teach, why would she think she would be happy doing something else just because the schooling for something else may be quicker? Thinking about this statement is sad to me.

Don't be like this young woman. Commit to living your best life no matter how long it takes. You'll be happier, more successful, and more fulfilled. Neither settle nor give up on the achievement of your goal. Instead, set yourself up for success and break those goals into smaller steps. That way your goal won't seem too overwhelming for you—and you will know easily where to start. You can do it! You just have to be-live in yourself!

Your Turn

- Determine what your goals are and then break down your goals into smaller steps. Write down the smaller steps (chunking).

- Transfer your smaller steps onto index cards.

- Post your index cards all over your house and your car if you can.

- Make your cell phone screensaver a constant reminder of your goals.

- See yourself achieving your goals—use your blessed imagination! Take a few minutes each day reflecting on your goals. I have an alarm labeled and set throughout the day to remind me to be "present and conscious" about a particular goal. It's a great feeling!

- I have labeled and set alarms on my cell phone to go off during different parts of the day as a time for reflection about my goals.

- Advertise to yourself, be your own big marketing agency.

- Get out the scissors, markers, and glue, and create a dream board.

- This one is only if you're really serious about your goal(s): write your goal down on paper, then address the envelope to yourself, put a stamp on it, and give it to someone whom you trust and respect. Ask them to mail it to you exactly one year from the date you wrote it. When you get it in the mail, you can see just how far you have come. I have done this a few times.

A "PS" on Dream Boards

Have fun making your dream board! Get out the magazines, crayons, markers, and anything else that is going to be a part of your project. This is also a good project you can work on with kids if you have them. Make them with your children for their rooms. Have them write their dreams while you're working on yours. I remember I did a dream board with my son. He was so excited to put all his dreams on a board.

Big agencies do this all the time too. It is how they find creative ways to get people to purchase their items. Why can't you advertise to yourself as much as they advertise to you? Trust me, it's fun.

Chapter 11

Funding Your Dreams

An investment in knowledge pays the best interest.
—Benjamin Franklin

If you don't know how to properly use or manage your money, it will result in you being unable to achieve your goals. What most people lack in this process is the knowledge of how to handle their money. I will explain the importance of managing your money correctly and show why it is extremely important.

King Cash

Here is my experience with cash: when you have cash in your wallet or purse, you manage your money a little differently. Because you can look at the money, because you can physically see how much you actually have left sitting in your wallet, you are much more careful in spending it. Additionally, having cash at your disposal is a huge benefit because you have the ability to bargain with the seller and make deals with people who have cash at their disposal. A simple example of this is when you go to get fuel. At some gas stations, the sign has separate cash and credit card prices.

The direct opposite happens when you use debit or credit cards. When you get into the habit of using a card, you can easily keep swiping your cards without an awareness of how much you are really spending. Then you can get locked in the downward spiral of paying interest if you are using credit cards and carrying a balance. If you use a debit card with no balance, you will be subject to overdraft penalties.

The credit card companies love it when you use your credit cards and carry a balance. They are aware that people who use debit or credit cards are typically not conscious purchasers. This is how credit card companies make their money.

Credit card debt can be extremely dangerous to your well-being. I remember attending college with a person whose father committed suicide because the debt was out of control.

Unconscious vs. Conscious Spending

Here is a common example of unconscious and conscious purchasing:

Whenever you go to a restaurant, for example, and the cashier asks if you want to "supersize" for thirty-nine cents more, if you are paying with a card, you automatically agree most of the time. However, if you are paying with cash and you look into your wallet and see that you don't have the thirty-nine cents, you will say no. So, using cash will not only save you money but also save your waistline!

Piggy Bank Power

Decide on an amount that will be your allowance and stick to it. Find yourself two Mason jars, one for cash and one for coins. If you give yourself a sixty-dollar a week allowance for your incidentals (or the amount you deem fit), whatever is left in your wallet on Sunday gets thrown into the jars. Then, on Monday go to your bank and take out your next allotment of the sixty-dollar allowance. Try to keep practicing this exercise for the rest of your life.

Once you see your Mason jars growing, you can use that money for something you've been saving up for. The reason behind the Mason jars is because they are pretty sturdy and last forever. Plus, seeing your money grow in clear jars inspires you to keep saving. You will be surprised at how easy it is to save money this way.

Now, sometimes you may want to use all that accumulated Mason jar money to purchase something on the Internet, which is fine. Just remember to immediately pay off your card. Better yet, use a PayPal account. It is hooked up to your bank account. You can take the money from your jar, deposit it into your bank account, and then use PayPal to purchase that plane ticket to Hawaii you have been wanting for so long.

You really are in control of your finances, even if it doesn't seem like it. It is not how much you make, but rather, how much you keep that matters.

The Awe of Automaticity

Set up automatic deposits of your paycheck into your checking and savings accounts to help lower the temptation of spending it. If you get a check and go cash it, then you will be tempted to keep some and spend it. Automatic deposits into your accounts will save you from this temptation and save you time. Do you remember back when I talked about multiplying your time? Well, here's another example. This way, you won't have to wait in line with everyone else to cash your check.

Also, you can set your direct deposit to automatically divide the deposited money into parts and put one part in the checking account and another part in your savings account. For example, assume the direct deposit is for $1,000. You can set it up to put $100 in your savings account and $800 in your checking account. Then you go to another institution, open a separate savings account, and have your company put the final $100 there. You can live off the $800, and if you need money for an emergency, you can get cash from your savings account that is in the same institution as your checking account.

The beauty of having another savings account in a separate institution is that it is harder to get your hands on the cash. It takes a lot more effort. Also, what is out of sight is out of mind. This separate savings account will keep growing because you're not able to touch it as easily as you would if it were in the same institution as your checking account.

I do recommend that the second savings account should be set up in a credit union, so if one day when you do need to replace that used car or purchase a home, you have a relationship with a credit union, which is typically smaller and more personable than a bank. Often credit unions' interest rates are much lower too.

More Money = More Debt. What?

I have personally seen people with a large amount of income, and their money goes straight to their lifestyle— buying more and more things and even going into debt because of it. These people can never afford to take their kids on vacations because all their money is tied up in their house and all the toys they buy. Not to mention the stress it puts on the entire family.

There is nothing wrong with having some toys and buying some nice things here and there, but if you're nice things start to get in the way of your goal, that is when it becomes a problem. Yes, I've already addressed this point previously in chapter 8, "The Killer Combo," but it is so important and such a common mistake that I think it is necessary to revisit it.

Remember the difference between "need" and "want"; needing something is a lot different than wanting it. When an item is considered a necessity, this means it is something we cannot physically live without. Wanting, on the other hand, is something a person is craving and wishes to have, but does not need.

For Parents—Money and Your Children

Train up a child in the way that he should go: and when he is old, he will not depart from it.
—Proverbs 22:6

As a parent, I think co-signing for a car loan is a mistake. When co-signing with your kids to get a new or used car, you actually put them behind because now they have a financial obligation to pay a car payment. Remember, when you sign your name to anything, you are signing a written promise! If something should happen to you or your income and you can no longer help your child pay the car note, this leaves your child buried with debt they may not be able to pay on their own. A poor credit score is something that will hinder both the child and the parents for a very long time. Remember, too, that the interest rate represents how well you have kept your word. Difficulty paying off a car loan will affect not only your credit score but theirs too.

I have seen youngsters get so stressed out about making car payments and higher insurance premium payments because of the decision to purchase a car. Now remember, this isn't the only side effect of getting into debt for a vehicle. I have seen students not only very stressed, but terribly tired and distracted from studying and doing their best in school or at work all because of huge car-related payments.

I'm not against students having jobs. They should work a little to gain the experience of having a job and handling finances. They even appreciate their things more when there is a little sweat equity involved. I just don't believe it is in their best interest to be saddled with debt when they are that young.

My children weren't exactly thrilled at the time when I didn't buy them a car like their friends got during high school. But now, as young adults, they appreciate that they are not like their peers—burdened with the debt of a car payment and high insurance premiums. My son recently shared with me how he is not as stressed as some of his friends are and how he is able to actually enjoy his paycheck. This is why I never let my kids buy a brand-new car when they reached driving age.

As parents, we can utilize a Mason jar for our teenager's first car. I have been fortunate enough to purchase cars for cash when I bought them, for all three of my kids. I told them that I would match what they were able to save, so they never had to worry about car payments or astronomical insurance costs. It really is possible to purchase a decent car from anywhere for three to five thousand dollars. Plus, when you have cash in your hands, you have more leverage with the seller of the car.

Your Turn

- Open up a checking account and a savings account in one bank. At another bank, set up a savings account.

- Set up your paycheck to automatically deposit in the checking and two savings accounts.

- Purchase a couple of Mason jars and start giving yourself a weekly cash allowance. Put the leftovers in the appropriate jar—bills or coins.

- Sign up for a PayPal account.

- Choose to be a conscious spender and teach your children to be conscious about their spending and saving too.

- Value your time more than you value new stuff. Only when you achieve big goals and milestones should you reward yourself with that special gift you've been eyeing.

Chapter 12

Got Benefits?
Explore the Possibilities:
401K, Stocks, and Your Future

A journey of a thousand miles begins with a single step.
—Lao Tzu

For those of you out there who have a job that offers a 401K program, make sure to take advantage of it. Investing in a 401K will give you lots of great options.

The 401K will take your pre-taxed income and will usually invest it in mutual funds, stocks, bonds, CDs, real estate, and more. What's great is that typically you can decide how much risk you want the investment to entail. If you are averse to risk, you can allocate that money to very stable investments, like CDs or bonds. If you don't know where you stand or simply feel confused by the whole thing, you can speak to a consultant at the investment firm associated with your 401K. It is their job to help you understand the 401K and all your options, so don't hesitate to ask every single question you have to get clear. You are the client, so you deserve answers.

Over time, the money you put in your 401K is supposed to grow with the market. That way, years later when you can't work as much, you can withdraw that money and it is a much larger amount than what you put in yourself.

The Money Match

Most organizations have an offer in place that if you contribute a particular amount to your 401K, the organization will match a percentage of the amount you contribute. What this means essentially is they will give you money if you opt for it. Say, for example, that your organization agrees to match monthly contributions up to four percent in an employee's 401K. What this means is that if you put in the minimum amount required by your company, then the company will also match a certain percentage. You can find out more about how your organization's 401K plan works by contacting your benefits department.

Pay Less Taxes Too

As I said, the money that you put in the 401K is pre-taxed money. This is great because not only will you be investing and growing your money in the 401K, you'll also be paying less tax on your yearly income. For example, if you make $50K per year and you invested $7K in your 401K, the government only considers that you earned $43K. So you are taxed like a $43K-earner. This is fabulous because it means you pay less money in taxes.

Even More Possibilities

I have seen some of my coworkers borrow against their 401Ks to purchase their first homes. Of course, you must pay yourself back or else you'll have to pay a severe penalty. But it is still great to have this option rather than having to borrow from a bank, borrow from a family member, or simply not have the money to buy the home at all.

You can also simply let the money in the 401K grow and eventually use it to fund part of your kid's college tuition or your retirement.

Notice I wrote "part"? I emphasize "part" because I strongly believe that when a person has to pay for part of their college tuition, they appreciate their education more and try harder to successfully pass their classes. At least, this is what I have experienced personally and what I've witnessed over the years among those employees who have had to pay for their own classes.

You must talk to your benefits department or accountant to learn more about the 401K plan. This type of savings is good for those people who want to make it automatic. As with direct deposit, you can set it up with your employer for a certain amount of each paycheck to automatically go in your 401K. Then you don't have to think about it or see it. You will receive a quarterly statement that will show you how you are doing in the market along with your balance. You can also follow your 401K account through the Internet. This is only one way to fund your dreams of sending your kids to college, purchasing your new home, or having a retirement fund.

Stocks

Stock trading is another investment strategy. A stock is a share and part ownership in a company. Some stocks pay dividends that you can choose to reinvest. There are many ways to participate in the stock market. You can go online and purchase stocks through Etrade, Ameritrade, and many other brokerage firms.

You can also go to your financial institution and purchase stocks through the local broker. Once you set up an appointment with the local stockbroker, you can talk to them about your investment goals. Just to be clear, you should expect to be charged a fee through an online trading company or a stockbroker as that is how they earn money and commissions.

My Investing Experience

I was very fortunate to have Lem Poates, whom I wrote about in the chapter about the importance of mentors, as my supervisor. Lem insisted that I didn't spend any of my bonus check that he handed me until I met with his stockbroker. I took his advice because I respected him and he had credibility with me. I did what he recommended, and I can say that I have continued to have a relationship with his stockbroker for close to twenty years.

I have been making automatic deposits into my stock account for several years now. I like having everything done automatically if I am able. This way it is one less thing for me to think of, and it also saves me time. I personally learned a lot on the "automatic strategy" from reading *Automatic Millionaire* by David Bach. You already know how much I advocate reading!

The company I work for had a stock option benefit, which I cashed in once it matured. I used this money to fund a portion of my real estate goals. I was able to use part of my stock options to purchase a rental property. I got into real estate after reading *Rich Dad Poor Dad* by Robert Kiyosaki. Let me say it again—read, read, read!

Notice that I cashed in an investment simply to make another investment. I grew money, harvested the money, and used the harvest to grow even more money. Just as I advocate reading, I advocate spending to grow yourself first—and only the occasional toy later.

My point is that investing in stocks and other investing options offered at the workplace has benefited me greatly. I've been making some nice extra income from my investments. I tell you this to inspire and encourage you to invest too.

Your Turn

- Head over to your benefits department and get to know your benefits.

- If you don't understand your options, ask questions or go online and become familiar with the terms or language. I like www.smartmoney.com because it has all kinds of information about money, and it is pretty easy to understand.

- Keep a journal of all the new investment terms that you are learning.

- Go to the library or go online and pick up *Automatic Millionaire* by David Bach or *Rich Dad Poor Dad* by Robert Kiyosaki. Read and learn— and read more!

Chapter 13

The eBay Opportunity: Money and Skills

The way to get started is to quit talking and begin doing.
—Walt Disney

Cash Gains—And More

I like eBay because there have been times when something unexpected came up, and I didn't want to use my credit card. I then decided to clean out some of the closets in my house and sell some items on eBay. I'd already gotten the benefit from them, so by selling them, I was providing someone else the opportunity to purchase them at a fraction of the cost.

One time, I was actually able to raise enough money from selling things on eBay that I was able to pay for the fuel injectors I needed to repair my truck.

In addition to the obvious—getting some cash—I believe you are going to gain some sales, marketing, and customer service experience by using eBay. Let me explain what I mean.

The Essential Skills

The items you are going to sell on eBay have to be in the best condition possible if you are going to command a high selling price. First, you have to prepare your product. This means you must have it ready to sell. You must take appealing pictures of it to post to your potential buyers. Then you must write a description of what you are trying to sell.

Next, you have to market your item. This means making it appealing and enticing to potential buyers. Of course, how you prepare your product in the photos and description certainly plays into the marketing of the item. One way you can figure out how to market it is to study how other sellers of similar items write their descriptions. You can take what others have written and personalize or paraphrase it. Also you can find tutorials and videos on eBay to help you become a successful seller. You can use these tools to market your item. Over time you will gain important skills in research to develop your own ad for the product you are selling on eBay.

The reason you gain customer service experience is because you will have to communicate with the person who buys your item. Through these communications, you learn how to be professional, helpful, and influential. For example, once your item sells, you are going to package it and mail it to the buyer. If you put the item in the box and ship it off to the buyer, that is acceptable, but it is also average and not next level. What I encourage you to do is write a small thank you note (notice I said write and not type), thanking them for purchasing your item and asking them to please provide feedback on their transaction. Make sure to sign the note. A handwritten letter is always more personable and courteous than a typed note.

The feedback you will receive will help to improve your selling strategy on eBay. You will also notice that the more positive the feedback you receive, the more stars you get. These stars indicate that you are a trustworthy seller. You want to be known as a trustworthy seller, so you can sell more. Being trustworthy also includes refunding any extra shipping fees to the buyer if they were over-charged.

If you ever receive a complaint, make it right. Refund the money if you must. You ultimately are a business on eBay, and your name is the brand. Although you are technically a seller, I don't want you to see yourself that way, but rather as a business. After all, that is what you are. I have had to refund a few people in the past, and I didn't take it personally. Instead, I improved and moved on. This is all part of gaining important customer service and small business skills.

One Last Note of Encouragement

I believe that a cluttered closet is just as bad as a cluttered mind. What I mean by this is that if you have things you don't use anymore, that stuff is just taking up space when it could be serving others. I call this "use value."

This is how I see it: if an item that you no longer want is stored in your closet, then it is taking up space. Someone else could be benefitting from it. You have already enjoyed it, and if you took care of it, then you can easily sell it on eBay. You will not just gain some extra cash, but you will also be making someone else happy. You see, it is a win-win situation. Your closet, garage, or cupboard now has space for something else, in addition to a little cash in your pocket. There is nothing wrong with that, right?

You can use the extra cash from your eBay account to help with other goals you have. If you are able to see eBay as a way to gain experience in marketing, selling, and customer service, then not only do you gain a little more cash flow, but you also make gains in your own personal development and skillset. Wow! That's exactly what I'm trying to teach you in this book!

Your Turn

- Sign up for an eBay account.

- Take some of the tutorials to become successful on eBay.

- Sign up for a PayPal account because this is how you will get paid.

- Check out the back of this book for some additional money-making tips.

Chapter 14

The Art of Real Estate

It's tangible, it's solid, it's beautiful. It's artistic, from my standpoint, and I just love real estate.
—Donald Trump

Passive income has been a long-term goal of mine. There is nothing better than having your money working for you. So far, real estate has been one of my favorite ways of earning passive income. The mortgage property taxes and interest are paid by the tenant, and the remaining balance is yours to reinvest, whether it be to save, to fund smaller goals, or to purchase whatever you desire.

The one thing I have discovered in pursuing this goal is that once you do anything one time, you have the recipe to do it again. All you have to do is follow the ingredients, and you can create more money. This is also why I recommend finding a mentor because a mentor with experience in this area can provide great guidance.

Right now, let me share with you some of the essential ingredients I've learned in my recipe for real estate success.

Your First Home Purchase

Instead of purchasing a single-family home, I recommend that friends and family look into purchasing a duplex or triplex. I believe that purchasing a multi-unit home allows you to gain the experience of becoming a landlord. Plus, if you live in one unit and have a duplex or triplex, you have one or two other people helping you pay the mortgage.

My advice is to move in and learn how to manage a rental property because it will only benefit you in the long run. You can also hire a property manager, but what better experience than actually doing it yourself?

Once you gain enough equity in that property, you can turn it around within a few short years and purchase another one if you desire. You can even purchase your single-family home at that later time. So this way, you now basically have your rentals helping you to pay off your mortgages.

Choosing the Best Location

Have you ever heard, "Location, location, location"? Well, guess what? Location is, in fact, everything. When you purchase your rental property in the right location, you usually won't have a problem keeping your property rented.

I purchase homes I would want to live in myself. With that said, here are some things to help you determine if the location is right for you—which means right for your tenants. First, look for locations and neighborhoods where the homes look like people care about them. You can tell a lot about a family or neighborhood just by looking at how they take care of their lawns and yards.

Check out the potential rental property during different times in the day. If you go at night and the neighborhood is full of partying neighbors, you will probably lose good families who won't be able to get rest at night due to all the noise.

Look for a great school district as well. You might want to check out the schools and know how they rank in academics. This is a great selling point to remember because the bottom line is you are always selling. Also, you want to know or figure out where all the nearest stores are in the town; this matters.

Location, location, location—it is everything in real estate. Just to ensure you understand, I'll repeat: location is everything!

Homework

You should always run your rental property like a business. This way you are coming at it from a professional standpoint. If you do your homework upfront, your rental property or investment properties should all run smoothly. An important piece of homework is in-person interviews with potential tenants as well as complete background and reference checks.

I highly recommend interviewing the potential tenants. I have set up meetings at the local Starbucks for this, and you can use this method as well. In addition to the normal credit and reference checks, I always ask their previous landlord the following question: "If the Jones family were to move back to your city, would you rent to them again?" When the landlord responds with silence, it is not a good sign. The silence is telling you to stay away from the potential tenant in most cases. I will not rent to anyone without doing a reference check first. Remember to always do the work upfront to eliminate potential headaches down the road.

I also call their personal references because even though the personal references may have prepared answers, there is still a lot you can tell by them. Because remember, "Birds of a feather flock together."

Contract

You will also write up a contract establishing the cleaning and security deposit expectations. These should be deposited into a rental savings account so that when the tenant leaves the property, you can give them back the balance after cleaning and repairing any agreed-upon items. Hopefully your tenants keep the property in great condition, so you can return their deposit in its entirety.

Neighbors

Once you purchase the property, I recommend going to your immediate neighbors and introducing yourself. I usually give them my contact information just in case there are any problems or if there is anything they may need. I always assure my neighbors that I am not a slumlord and that my property will remain in good condition. It puts the neighbors who do own their homes at ease to know I am a respectful and responsible landlord.

I recall a time when one of my neighbors from a rental house called me and was concerned about all the parked cars. I looked into it. Though the abandoned vehicle wasn't my tenants', I went to the local police department to report it. Having relationships with the neighbors of your rental property is a great thing and highly recommended for both parties.

Money On Hand

You should have on hand at least three months of actual mortgage payments in case your property is vacant for a period of time. Also, the money you hold for running the business can be used for cleaning between tenants.

Tax Benefits

You can also take advantage of the tax benefits of being a landlord. You can write off some items, such as mileage, going to and from showings of your rental property, interviewing potential tenants, and visiting the property monthly. Preparing the property for rental and the cleaning supplies you use can be written off in most cases. If you prefer, you can hire a property management company, which can be written off as well.

Here is a reminder about the job you have as a landlord. I have gained so much experience interviewing my employees. Now that I have gained this skill, I can easily and successfully interview potential tenants. Never despise those small beginnings in your work life because you never know where they may lead you. As I've said before, with an open and eager mind, you can learn and grow from almost any experience—and put those new skills to work for you in another context. It's all about your attitude and commitment—choose to succeed and take action.

Your Turn

- Play Monopoly. I'm not kidding—it's fun and it helps you understand real estate: four greenhouses equal one red hotel.

- Read books on real estate and becoming a landlord because you must become familiar with the language. Remember when I said every industry has a language? Here are my book recs:

  Rental Houses for the Successful Small Investor by Suzanne P. Thomas

  The Book on Managing Rental Properties by Brandon Turner

  Real Estate Riches by Dolf de Roos and Robert T. Kiyosaki

- Find other landlords and interview them. Ask them what they like and dislike about being a landlord.

Call a couple of real estate offices, and let them know you are interested in an "investment" property. You must call a few and work with someone whom you feel comfortable with.

Remember—this is your business.

Chapter 15

Never Be Afraid to Be-Live

If I have the belief that I can do it, I shall surely acquire the capacity to do it even if I may not have it all at the beginning.
—Mahatma Ghandi

I used to say, "Be, do, have," but then after years of studying and examining this relationship, I discovered another way to explain "belief"—be it, do it, and have it. While I introduced this notion in chapter 10, "Got Goals?" I want to delve farther into the "be-live" philosophy. It's a concept of living that was pivotal in my life, and I want it to work for you in the same way.

The How-To of "Be-live"

This may sound crazy, but I believe you must physically put yourself into the particular situations you hope to be the norm for yourself in the future. It is sort of like window-shopping—when you go to the mall or a store and just drool over the items you desire. Let me give you some examples.

I can't even tell you how many times I drove to La Jolla, CA, just to sit in a Starbucks and take in the feeling of being in a nice city around professionals from other industries. I would literally just sit there, reading and people-watching.

Another example: I have sat in nice hotel lobbies people-watching to build my confidence in regard to what is possible in life. I believe success leaves clues for you. You are able to see what successful people are doing, how they walk, how they speak to one another, and what they are wearing. In some instances, I have even struck up conversations with these people. In this way, I have gained access to the clues.

Don't think what I'm proposing is some wild idea I'm making up off the top of my head. I have read a number of books on faith and belief, for example, *The Magic of Thinking Big* by David J. Schwartz, *As a Man Thinketh* by James Allen, and, of course, the Bible—all are full of examples. My "be-live" philosophy—be it, do it, and have it—stemmed from my personal research. I see it as another very effective strategy to get yourself out of your comfort zone and into the growth zone.

I see this practice of physically immersing myself in the spaces of successful people as a kind of personal expansion. You are best served by finding places where you and your mind can expand. Just like a balloon that stretches when it is filled with air, once that air is released, the balloon is never the same again because it expanded. That is exactly what happens when you spend time around people who are doing and living the life you wish to be living—you'll never be the same again because you've been expanded.

It is not that you are envious of them; it is that by nature you want more out of life. You can achieve more of the things you desire if you follow these few steps to build up your "be-live" muscles. People-watching, taking in the clues, and wondering are for your imagination. It is just one step you can follow to begin the process of obtaining more.

Some Be-Live Exercises

Let me share a few more examples of how to build up your "be-live" muscles. As I already shared, you can go to a coffee shop in the nicest part of town. There, you can buy a cup of coffee and take in the ambiance, the feeling that you belong. Notice the people and your surroundings. Go to the best hotel. Although you may not be able to stay there, you can go to one of the hotel's restaurants and order soup and salad. This is a good expansion exercise as well.

Go to a nice department store. I remember the first time I went to Saks 5th Avenue, and they were having a shoe sale. I tried on several pairs of shoes, and even though I wasn't going to purchase them, I did it to build my "be-live" muscle. The expansion exercise was successful, and, today, I am happy to say that I can now shop at Saks 5th Avenue if I desire to.

Two Important Side Notes

One—Get yourself into a position where you don't always have to purchase the least expensive items. When continually purchasing cheap, you train your mind that all you can afford is that. Never say you cannot afford something. Instead, say that you "prefer not to" purchase it at the time. While this may seem small and unimportant, what it comes down to is self-empowerment. You empower yourself and create more confidence when you phrase it "prefer not to" rather than "cannot." And remember—each step of confidence builds and builds to propel you down the road of possibility and success.

Two—I've said this already in this book, but I want to say it again: never say that you are "poor." Even when I was financially challenged as a single mother with two kids, I never called myself "poor." Why would you want to say that to yourself? Especially out loud? Remember what I said about advertising to yourself? Again, in labeling yourself as "poor," you take away from yourself power and possibility.

Instead say only positive things about yourself and your life. Imagine the life you want to live, and speak about what you want in your life. That way you open yourself up to achievement and possibility. Don't talk about what you don't have in your life. That kind of negative talk reinforces a can't-do attitude.

Your Turn

- Go to a nice restaurant, order soup and salad with a glass of water with lemon. Take in that feeling, and notice what people are wearing, how they speak, and their behavior. Don't rush this homework assignment. Enjoy it!

- Go to a nice hotel and sit in the lobby. Check out their coffee shop, and do the same as the first practice.

- Go to a nice department store, check things out, and take notice of the displays. You can even try on some shoes or clothes. You don't have to buy anything—this is just for fun. So, go on and blow up like a balloon!

- Go test-drive a nice car. I recommend looking online first and learning a thing or two about the vehicle, so when you go on the test-drive, you will be knowledgeable about it. Have the salesperson take a picture of you in the car. It doesn't cost anything but time, and well-invested time at that.

PICTURE OF LORI IN MERCEDES

Lori test-driving a Mercedes in 2003. She opted for the pre-owned BMW instead.

A "PS" on the "Your Turn"

The above assignments are designed to get you out of your comfort zone. You must exercise your "be-live" muscles in order to strengthen the "be-live" part of your goals. If you see someone who is successful in an area you aspire to be successful in, you can approach this in three ways: (1) ask them if they would be willing to mentor you,

(2) ask them if they know someone they would recommend to mentor you, or (3) just observe them.

When I say "observe," I mean watch them just like you would watch television. See how they conduct themselves in public. What do they eat? What do they read? What are their hobbies? How do they move? How do they talk to others? You can really learn a lot by paying attention to these things.

As I stated before, success leaves clues.

Notice how successful people dress a certain way. You too can dress like that. If you are unable to purchase what they are wearing, don't worry. Start from where you're at. Check out thrift or discount stores. It is amazing how you will feel by dressing the part.

Dressing the part is like getting into character. I remember as a little girl that putting on my mom's high heels made me instantly feel like I was extravagant. This is equivalent to landing a role in a play, getting into costume, and character acting like someone you are not. But as you do it more and more, it becomes who you are. You will always perform to that image you have for yourself, so make that image the self you want to be. Make it your ideal self. Be-live in yourself!

Chapter 16

Essence of Everything

The good life is one inspired by love and guided by knowledge.
—Bertrand Russell

In the beginning of this book, I used the example of a personal trainer in hopes that you could see the parallels between building your body and building your mind. This book is your very own personal trainer for getting you to your next level and not staying stuck in the position you are in today.

This book is packed with examples, practices, and actionable items for you to get unstuck in your own life. When coming across the "Your Turn" sections, you must take action. Belief without action is useless. In other words, you must put action behind your desires. Your desires will not magically appear or fall from the sky. You must invest some time and energy, just as you would when going to the gym.

When you face difficulties at the gym and backtrack, your personal trainer is there to lift you back up. When backtracking in life, this book is here to lift you back up. If you would like, please visit my website, www.loricw.com, as it is my desire to assist you in getting to your next level.

You will always get out of life what you put into it. This principle is a law that I didn't make up. Some people call this, "sowing and reaping," and others call it, "cause and effect." I could have easily stayed stuck in the many circumstances I have landed in. Then my life would have turned out very differently, and you would not be reading this book today.

I don't care if you are a single mom, a high-school dropout, or a former whatever it is you might be: *don't stay stuck!* You can accomplish your goals and dreams. While the path may not be a straight line—it seldom ever is. Don't let the path become more important than your destination. Remember—you were born a winner!

Growing up, I did not have my dad, and the relationship with my mother was strained. As a result of the combination of events in my life, I didn't always make the best choices. Notice I said "I"; always remember that blaming others for problems in your life is what keeps you stuck.

For years I was betting on a horse named Self-Pity. It was a race the horse was never going to win. You see, similar to a racetrack where you go round and round, some of you are experiencing your own horse race, and guess what? As long as you stay stuck, betting on that horse of Doubt, Worry, or even Fear, you will never win.

For years, I thought I was going to be stuck in a race, going in circles and never gaining any traction. Looking back from where I started this journey and where I stand today, I now realize that all the mistakes and poor choices I made in my life have just become lessons learned and chapters that I have grown from. Although I am still in the race, I am no longer stuck. I am now betting on a horse named Champion. I am betting that this horse is a winner because I am no longer stuck on the track. I have been training my "be-live" muscles, the gates have been opened, and I am free and ready to run my own race.

I've given you the examples, practices, actionable items, and personal stories from my life, so you can place your bets on Champion too. Go for it. "Be-live" in yourself!

Answering the Call
A Life with No Regrets

As I continue "be-living" my life, I also continue to amaze and inspire myself each and every day to live life to the fullest. Although I have had my fair share of setbacks and many negative events have occurred, I continue to see the best in life.

We only have one life to live, so we must live it to the fullest, to the maximum of our abilities. This book is not only teaching you how to get unstuck, but it is also teaching you to become a better goal-chaser and achiever. This book also reminds me why I made the decision to not stay stuck in my life.

As I close, I would like to leave you with this: as you know, this book is about more than how to rise above your fears and circumstances. It's about you getting yourself unstuck and reaching your next level. In fact, it is totally for your next level. When I started this journey to put my thoughts and ideas on paper, I was solely thinking of you, the reader, and providing ideas and strategies, so you could create an additional income stream or two.

As I listened to my coach, RE Vance, encouraging me to "bleed" on the pages, and to Chandler Bolt of Self-Publishing School, telling me to write a letter to one person in my target audience that I want to inspire, it turned into this—a book that I hope will ignite you to take the necessary actions to get yourself to your next level—for life—whatever it may be.

When you apply excellence and a great work ethic to all that you do, there really is no reason why you should not achieve your next level in all areas of your life.

I congratulate you for taking the time to invest in yourself and your future. Once you get to the point in life where you continue to amaze and inspire yourself each and every day, you will not only have accomplished your dreams, but I will have accomplished mine.

I encourage you to e-mail me at loricwysocki@gmail.com with your testimonials and stories about how this book has helped you. Your message will be a testimony that my taking the risk of putting a piece of my life out in the open for others to view was worth it.

For those of you writing to share your stories on how this book has helped you, please put "red balloon" in the subject line. Why? Because this lets me know that you indeed read this book. The balloon represents your expansion, all that you have learned from reading this book.

If you enjoyed reading my book, I would so appreciate it if you would spread the word about *Don't Stay Stuck*. I am grateful for your time and energy providing me with feedback.

For your convenience, I have provided my e-mail, loricwysocki@gmail.com, and website at www.loricw.com.

Here's to you achieving your next level,

Lori Chavez-Wysocki

A Note to Parents

Some of you may have had a similar experience to mine of being called names and being ridiculed at school, or you may have known someone who has. Childhood can be a very stressful time for youngsters.

I am not a perfect mother by any means, but I have learned over the years that our children will rise to what we expect from them. If you encourage and support them, it is like depositing into their self-esteem account.

Think about the kid that goes to school who hasn't had any deposits made into his or her account and is called every unimaginable name at school. A kid like this comes home totally withdrawn for a reason.

Encourage your children by building them up. Use words, such as *amazing, champion, awesome, fantastic, winner*, etc. Remind them how beautiful they are on the inside, where it really counts. I cannot say I have always done this, but I have learned over the years as I have grown and developed that this is extremely important.

Do yourself and your kids a favor—see the champion in them. You will have them in your home for a very short period of time. If you wish to have an amazing relationship with them after they are gone, invest in building your relationship with them today. Go on and tell them how wonderful they are because, remember, the apple doesn't fall far from the tree!

Additional Resources

Fiverr and **Upwork** are very similar in that they both provide a platform where you can offer a variety of services. Maybe you know how to design a website, ghost write, or design a logo. On these platforms, you can advertise these services. When someone hires you to do some work, you will get paid. These sites offer great opportunities to gain exposure along with a little cash. Think about this—what if you designed a logo and the company or person you designed it for wants to put you on a contract? So do it with excellence! Go on.

Uber is another way for you to earn additional income. Uber is essentially a taxi service. The drivers use their own vehicles to provide paid rides to customers. The Uber company keeps five to twenty percent, and the remaining money is then deposited into the driver's account. The driver must pass a DMV background check. The driver must have their own car and must be fully insured. The Uber experience will be what you put into it. So go on, take it to the next level, and provide amazing service. By the way, you never know whom you will meet.

Airbnb is another non-traditional way to rent out your space and also book unique accommodations anywhere in the world. When traveling, you can rent an apartment for a night or two, or even a castle or a villa. Airbnb connects people to unique travel experiences. Airbnb is an easy way for you to monetize your extra space too if you decide to rent it out through the service. Go on and do the research!

Etsy is another way for you to market and sell your crafts. If you have a creative bent, you can sell your items on Etsy. A friend of mine sells jewelry. It's like having your own boutique without the traditional storefront.

With the above income alternatives you can turn your space, your car, or your skills into cash!

More Traditional Methods: You are probably familiar with the more traditional ways of earning extra income, like Avon, Mary Kay, Jafra, and several other network-marketing companies. Network marketing has been around for a while. You will have a sponsor to help you get started. The sponsor gets a commission based on your success. Bottom line is that there are many ways you can put some extra cash into your pockets, wallet, or handbag.

"I Am" Statements

Never say anything about yourself you do not
want to come true.
—Brian Tracy

Here are a few examples of "I am" statements:

I am smart.

I am confident.

I am talented.

I am gifted in x.

I am uplifting towards others.

I am a great employee.

I am a great supervisor.

I am a compassionate person.

I am love.

I am healthy.

I am pretty.

I am powerful.

I am a great daughter.

I am a great father/mother.

I am a great leader.

I am wealthy.

I am wise with x.

I am flexible.

I am generous.

I am an encourager.

I am a money magnet.

I am a world changer.

I am a great student.

I am a great teacher.

I am a great x.

Remember that these are your statements. Say them aloud to yourself.

Here are two of mine that have become natural for me to say and that I believe:

"I am a world changer." When I started saying this, it was tough to say. However, as I would help a person out here and there, it became evident that I was a world changer. If I can inspire one person to make a positive change, then the dynamics of the world have changed; thus, I am a world changer. And guess what? You are too!

"I am a money magnet" is something I've been saying for years. I didn't believe this at first either, but when I would find change in the street, I would pick it up and say, "I am a money magnet." Over time this muscle got stronger.

A few years back, when my husband and I took a vacation to New York, I found a dollar, said something like, "I am a dollar richer," and thanked God. A few days later we took the subway to a baseball game and when I stepped through the turnstile, I stepped on a bill. I picked it up, looked around, and no one was there to claim it. I put it in my pocket. Later, I pulled it out and saw that it was a hundred-dollar bill. Again I gave thanks and, of course, did the happy dance. After the game, you would not believe what happened—we took the subway and started walking back to the hotel, and there was a twenty-dollar bill with some pennies lying in the street. *I am a money magnet!*

Be grateful for the small beginnings because you never know when the big ones will hit. Have you ever heard a person say, "Well, I'll start when x . . ."? X is never going to happen if you don't start at the level you are currently at. So, yes, when I find a penny, I say, "I'm a penny richer," and give thanks.

Go on and pick a couple of "I am" statements to start building those muscles.

Failures or Obstacles Provide Clarity

Here is another tool to provide clarity about what you desire rather than about what you are experiencing. It is another way to help you build your personal "I am" statements.

My Ideal Body

Contrast	Clarity
~~Flabby~~	Toned
~~Sluggish~~	Energetic
~~Overweight~~	Perfect weight

Examples:

I am extremely flexible and toned.

I am extremely energetic and powerful.

I am the perfect weight, and my metabolism works perfectly too.

Once you create your "I am" statement, cross out the contrasting statement. It is best to keep your "I am" statements in front of you, so you can review them often.

Then, before you know it, you will believe and achieve what it is that your heart desires.

Some Books That Have Shaped My Life

The Bible

The 7 Habits of Highly Effective People by Stephen R. Covey

See You at the Top by Zig Ziglar

The 21 Irrefutable Laws of Leadership by John C. Maxwell (Plus, all the books by this author!)

Reconciliation: Healing The Inner Child by Thich Nhat Hanh

First, Break All The Rules by Marcus Buckingham and Curt Coffman

The Magic of Thinking Big by David J. Schwartz

Raving Fans: A Revolutionary Approach to Customer Service by Ken Blanchard and Sheldon Bowles

Eleven Rings: The Soul of Success by Phil Jackson and Hugh Delehanty

The Secret of the Ages by Robert Collier

The Four Agreements by Don Miguel Ruiz and Janet Mills

Living with Joy by Sanaya Roman

The Alchemist by Paulo Coelho

Rich Dad Poor Dad by Robert Kiyosaki

The Science of Getting Rich by Wallace D. Wattles

The Slight Edge by Jeff Olson and John David Mann

Fish by Stephen C. Lundin and Harry Paul

Several titles from C. S. Lewis

Automatic Millionaire by David Bach

Post-Capitalist Society by Peter Drucker

How to Win Friends and Influence People by Dale Carnegie

Lori's Blessing Box

The blessing box is a great reminder full of cards, notes, and other small items that I have received over the years. No pity-party can withstand a blessing box.

About the Author

Lori Wysocki is an inspiration to all who aspire to become successful when feeling like they are stuck or at a dead-end job. Lori believes, "There is no such thing as a dead-end job," because she has gone from being a field worker to working the kitchen prep position to being a six-figure, award-winning district manager of eight Jack in the Box restaurants. During her eighteen-year career as a district manager, Lori has earned the coveted Circle of Excellence Award for Jack in the Box on six different occasions.

Although Lori was a teen-age mom and a high-school dropout, nothing has stopped this hardworking, self-educated woman from being successful. After dealing with a stressful and confusing childhood during which she witnessed her father drown to being in and out of foster care, Lori went on to attain her GED and later received her bachelor's degree in business administration, all the while being a fulltime mother of three.

Lori has also utilized her business degree and mindset to practice real estate. She worked as an adjunct instructor for the local community college. She's been invited to speak to various groups and organizations, including churches. She has excelled in these areas as well.

Lori has learned many ways to attain success through self-education. Lori enjoys teaching others life principles, beliefs, and habits to inspire them to find success at their entry-level jobs. Lori also wishes to motivate others to push through their struggles and become people that accomplish their goals, so they too can achieve their next level of success.

Lori believes, "We were all born a winner with a unique talent," and she knows that you can achieve success by investing time and effort because "what we put into life is what we get out of life."

RECOVERY ATTEMPT — Skin divers Dep. Cliff Arnhart, center, of the Big Bear Sheriff's substation, and Ronnie Trezise, Big Bear Lake Fire Dept. trainee, right, take a breather after trying to locate and recover the body of a fisherman who suffered a fatal heart attack and fell out of his boat. At left is Lt. Charles Follett, commander of the sheriff's substation, and an unidentified man. The body of the victim, Edward Kellar, of Inglewood, was later recovered by another team, Asst. Fire Chief John Poole and David Bushnell. —Eidson Photo

INGLEWOOD MAN STRICKEN WHILE BOATING ON LAKE

THURSDAY, Aug. 12
1 p.m.-5 p.m.; 7 p.m.-9 p.m.—Woman's Club Flower Show, clubhouse.
7:30 p.m. — BV Toastmistress Club, Rm. 18, Elementary school.

FRIDAY, Aug. 13
8 p.m.—Sportsman's Club, elementary school.

SATURDAY, Aug. 14
6 a.m. — Pancake Jamboree, Elks Barbecue grounds.
8 p.m.—Dancing Bears Square Dance, Woman's Clubhouse.

MONDAY, AUG. 16
7:30 p.m.—Big Bear Municipal Water District, Justice Court.

TUESDAY, Aug. 17
8 p.m.Vaqueros riding club, Vaqueros grounds.

Edward Kellar, 30, Inglewood, toppled from a boat into the lake 35 yards off shore Saturday, Aug. 7, a victim of a heart attack. He did not drown, as was first supposed. He was boating with his wife Marty and small daughter.

Hampered by heavy weed growth, rescue crews were not able to locate the body until 4:20 p.m.

A resuscitator was held in readiness while a crew of men from the Big Bear Lake Fire Dept., under Chief Larry Boyle, with volunteers manned five boats to drag the area just west of the Zebra Room where Kellar disappeared around 1:45 p.m. An underwater search was also made by skin divers Cliff Arnhart, deputy sheriff, and Ron Trezise, volunteer.

Recovery was finally made by Assistant Fire Chief John Poole and David Bushnell, volunteer, in approximately 15 feet of water. The body was turned over to Deputy Coroner Leo Reyes and transported to Mark B. Shaw Mortuary, San Bernardino, by Mountain Ambulance Service.

Five Lightning

The day that changed my life!

My mom and I, pictured above.

Look, Mom—I made it!

Made in the USA
San Bernardino, CA
24 May 2017